AF413703

# THE IRONIES OF FREEDOM

# THE IRONIES OF FREEDOM

WHEN PEOPLE USE **FREEDOM** AS A DEFENSE TO HARM OTHERS AND EVEN THEMSELVES

W. SHERMAN ROGERS

*The Ironies of Freedom:*
*When People Use FREEDOM as a Defense to Harm Others*
*and Even Themselves*



For information about this title or to order other books and/or electronic media, contact the publisher:

Colmar Publishing
# 1018 641 Avenue of the Americas
Front 2
New York, NY 10011

https://colmarpublishing.com
contact@colmarpublishing.com

ISBNs:
979-8-9892201-0-6 (hardcover)
979-8-9892201-1-3 (eBook)

Printed in the United States of America

# CONTENTS

# DETAILED TABLE OF CONTENTS

# PREFACE

*There is no higher value in American politics than freedom.* Yet, it is a highly contested concept. Indeed, persons—both individuals and entities—have used freedom and liberty-based arguments to suppress or even destroy the liberty rights of others throughout the history of the United States.

These same persons also seem willing to put themselves in harm's way in the name of freedom. They typically base their rationale on individual freedom against government paternalism, personal sovereignty to make final decisions about life and death, and the primacy of individual choice over public needs.

Consequently, many tolerate gun violence, an emerging climate disaster, a dangerous reduction in the social safety net, and a host of preventable injuries all in the name of freedom. Sometimes, they base their positions on the right to be free *from* government regulation. However, on other occasions, they justify policies that may even cause them harm on the freedom *to* engage in certain activities.

Columnist Fareed Zakaria, in a 2017 *Washington Post* article titled "The Populist Plutocrats March On," explored the reasons why people may support policies that may not be to their advantage. Zakaria observed that the most important revolution in economics in the past generation has been the rise of behavioral scientists, trained in psychology, *who are finding that people systematically make decisions that are against their own "interests."* The research, he noted, indicates that people may actually be motivated far more deeply by issues surrounding religion, race, and culture than they are by economics.

In Zakaria's view, these studies "might be the tip of the iceberg in understanding human motivation." The real story, he noted, might be that people see their own interests in a much more emotional and tribal way than scholars understand. Zakaria openly wondered whether, in the eyes of a large group of Americans, issues involving religion, race, and culture are the ones for which they will stand up, protest, support politicians, and even pay an economic price. Thus, Zakaria pondered whether "for many people, in America and around the world, these are their true interests[.]"

Interestingly, some organizations utilize freedom-based defenses to help their clients escape liability for conduct that adversely affects others. Those defenses include freedom of speech, freedom of religion, and other liberty-based constitutional protections. This is one of the many topics that we will address in this book. As freedom is intertwined in the discussion of so many political, historical, and economic issues, I have included a detailed table of contents in the book that will allow you to cherry-pick those topics you find most interesting.

A good illustration of the contested nature of what freedom means can currently be seen in the contrasting views of Florida governor Ron DeSantis and the editorial board of the *Washington Post*. On one hand, Florida governor Ron DeSantis refers to Florida as "a citadel of freedom," "freedom's linchpin," "freedom's vanguard," and "on the front lines of freedom." The editors of the *Washington Post*, however, see DeSantis' policies as a direct attack on freedom in Florida. In the *Post's* view, "Mr. DeSantis is waging frontal assaults on press freedom, reproductive freedom, free enterprise and academic freedom."

The *Post's* editors do not stop there. They also maintain that DeSantis, "in the name of protecting gun rights, has scaled back prudent safety rules" and is "now poised to target undocumented immigrants, including 'dreamers,' with what will be some of the cruelest policies in America."

An even more striking illustration of the contested nature of freedom can be seen in the Southern Poverty Law Center's June 2023 declaration that an organization called **Moms for Liberty** can be correctly labeled as an "extremist group" devoted to spreading "messages of anti-inclusion and hate," "conspiracy theories" and "actions to censor school discussions around race, discrimination, and LGBTQ+ identities."

The protection of the liberty rights of slave owners— and business owners generally—to engage in commercial activities without interference from a controlling federal government has been a prominent theme in American history. Consequently, there are frequent clashes between the desire of persons to be free of government regulation and the role of government to pass laws to protect society generally, as well as certain vulnerable members of society.

It only took 1 year and 45 days for contractors to build the Empire State Building from its March 17, 1930 starting date. However, it took Georgia 14 years to complete a $1 billion infrastructure project, largely because of environmental and regulatory hurdles. Regardless of one's political affiliation, it certainly appears that, in some instances, government regulation may be objectively excessive. And, while government regulation isn't intrinsically inefficient, it has occasionally created inefficiencies in the American economy.

Thus, it is quite understandable why some politicians and economists believe that government should eliminate many of the regulations that it imposes on businesses and entrepreneurs. In the view of some, when government intervenes in the market, it not only tramples on freedom and individual rights, but often hurts the very people it presumes to help. They believe, with few exceptions, that government regulatory programs, including social and welfare programs, impinge on the free market's ability to achieve maximum efficiency. Accordingly, in their view, unregulated market forces should determine economic outcomes—not the government. This requires that government not regulate any activity that encroaches on the ability of persons to enter into voluntary exchanges that are mutually acceptable to the parties to the bargain.

But the discussion of regulation tends to be much more complex. For example, artificial intelligence (AI) has the ability to dramatically improve life as we know it. However, there is now considerable research suggesting that AI has the ability to destroy humanity. This book discusses some of these alarming findings. Indeed, we are currently seeing some of the dark sides of AI. Nevertheless, some experts in the industry predict that no meaningful regulation will likely occur because of the money to be made by those with the ability to control the technology. Accordingly, regulation may only be forthcoming after a series of well-documented catastrophes occur. This is typically what must happen before regulation takes place in America. However, by then, it may be too late.

In the United States, the government has only enacted major economic and social welfare legislation as a matter of last resort. This is due, in part, to Americans' traditional suspicion of centralized power and authority. Thus, government regulation in the U.S. tends to be reactive and rarely proactive.

However, one need not take a normative stance on the ethics of those who use liberty-based defenses to recognize how they often deploy them—as a means to escape liability for harm they cause others. Yet, ironically, these defenders of freedom often take the position that the government should be able to prohibit the personal choices of others whose decisions are morally repugnant to their own beliefs.

It is noteworthy that Judeo-Christian teachings—upon which many of these defenders of freedom rely—explicitly place freedom of choice front and center. For example, God gave Adam and Eve the choice to break the rules even though they knew the long-term consequences. Therefore, it is interesting that the same persons who rely on these scriptures often use them to authorize the government to make choices against the will of other people when they find the conduct of these people to be morally unacceptable.

People, as a general proposition, do not like others to dictate to them what they can and cannot do—especially when it is the government that is mandating the prohibition. Instead, people generally want to have the right to make voluntary choices without government interference. However, the lack of rules often leads to chaos.

Therefore, a case can be made that government does not infringe on the freedom of persons and entities when it enacts targeted, smart, laws and regulations designed to assure the health and safety of its people in the least burdensome manner and when it spends a sufficient amount of the nation's revenues to maintain a viable social safety net for its inhabitants. On the other hand, there are those who believe that people should be able to voluntarily decide what they wish to do largely free of any government regulations and without any government-imposed social welfare programs.

This book explores the often-inconsistent premises that underly concepts of freedom and liberty. Ultimately, people must make a reasoned and informed choice on where they stand on these issues in a wide variety of contexts. We will discuss many of them in this book. It is for this reason that I have included a detailed table of contents in the book that will allow you to cherry-pick those topics you find most interesting.

I originally intended to publish this work as a law review article. However, I ultimately concluded that the work was more suitable for publication as a book. Therefore, I decided to search for a publisher who might be willing to publish the work as a book.

Accordingly, this book, much like a law review article, contains footnotes that adhere to the style manual known as the *Bluebook, A Uniform System of Citation*. This is the style manual that governs law review articles. However, unlike a law review article, the book contains a Preface, an Acknowledgments page, a Bibliography, and an Index that adhere to the *Chicago Style Manual*.

Additionally, the footnotes in the book, like footnotes in a law review article, run consecutively throughout the book—i.e., the footnotes in Part II will continue in chronological order from the footnotes in Part I. Similarly, the footnotes in Part III will continue in chronological order from Part II. The benefit of this approach is that it allows readers to easily cross-reference sources to the place where I originally cited them.

In the final analysis, I hope that you find this book—or at least a few of its passages—to be both illuminating and interesting.

# ACKNOWLEDGMENTS

*Many thanks to Howard University School* of Law Dean, Danielle Holley, for increasing the financial support awarded to faculty members to engage in scholarship on important legal, economic, and social issues. Best wishes to Dean Holley in her new position as the 20th President of Mount Holyoke College.

I would also like to give a special word of thanks to Colmar Publishing for making the financial commitment to publish this book. Additionally, many thanks to David Cavins for designing the cover of the book; 1106 Design, for providing interior design and layout services, indexing services, and overall project management in the production of this book. Additional thanks to Leila Whitlow for help with edits and Yvonne Rogers and Dr. Jeannette Rogers Dulan for their support and encouragement.

Finally, I would like to thank the folks at Ingram Content Group for their excellent work in the printing and distribution of this book.

All of these persons deserve praise for their role in helping to get this book out to the general public. However, I remain solely responsible for the content of this book and any matters that may arise from its publication.

# PART I
# INTRODUCTION AND OVERVIEW

$T$*his book explores how people and entities* often rely on notions of freedom, liberty, personal sovereignty, government sovereignty, and neoliberalism: (1) as defenses to their conduct regardless of whether it causes harm to others and (2) as grounds to avoid government regulation and liability for their actions.[1] Underlying the discussion are the frequent clashes between the desire of persons to be free of government regulation versus the role of government to protect society generally as well as certain vulnerable segments of society.

Ironically, persons have also used freedom and liberty-based arguments to suppress or even destroy the liberty rights of others throughout the history of the United States. They also seem willing to put themselves in harm's way in the name of freedom. Typically, they base their rationale on individual freedom against government paternalism, personal sovereignty to make final decisions about life and death, and the primacy of individual choice over public needs.

Consequently, many tolerate gun violence, an emerging climate disaster, a dangerous reduction in the social safety net, and a host of preventable injuries all in the name of freedom. Sometimes, they base their positions on the right

---

1 ELISABETH R. ANKER, UGLY FREEDOMS 1–16, 89 (2022). The term, "externality," refers to the actions of persons—both individuals and entities—that affect others. A negative externality exists when a person's acts affect others unfavorably and the person causing the harm does not pay the person harmed for the injury caused. A positive externality exists when a person's acts affect others in a favorable manner and the person receiving the benefit does not pay the person providing the benefit. JEFFREY L. HARRISON and JULES THEEUWES, LAW AND ECONOMICS 58–59 (2008). Most government regulation concerns efforts to respond to negative externalities. JEFFREY L. HARRISON, LAW AND ECONOMICS IN A NUTSHELL 328, 335 (5TH Ed. 2011). We discuss the topic of externalities in Part II and Part III of this book.

to be free *from* government regulation. However, on other occasions, they justify policies that may even cause them harm on the freedom *to* engage in certain activities.

Columnist Fareed Zakaria, in a 2017 *Washington Post* article titled *The Populist Plutocrats March On*, explored the reasons why people may support policies that may not be to their advantage. Zakaria observed that the most important revolution in economics in the past generation has been the rise of *behavioral scientists, trained in psychology, who are finding that people systematically make decisions that are against their own "interests."* The research, he noted, indicates that people may actually be motivated far more deeply by issues surrounding religion, race and culture than they are by economics.

In Zakaria's view, these studies "might be the tip of the iceberg in understanding human motivation." The real story, he noted, might be that people see their own interests in a much more emotional and tribal way than scholars understand. Zakaria openly wondered whether, in the eyes of a large group of Americans, issues involving religion, race, and culture are the ones for which they will stand up, protest, support politicians and even pay an economic price. Thus, Zakaria pondered whether "for many people, in America and around the world, these are their true interests[.]"

It is understandable why some politicians and economists believe that government should eliminate many of the regulations that it imposes on businesses, entrepreneurs, and people. In the view of some, when government intervenes in the market, it not only tramples on freedom and individual rights, but often hurts the very people it presumes to help. They believe, with few exceptions, that government regulatory programs, including social and welfare programs, impinge on the free market's ability to achieve maximum efficiency. Accordingly, in their view, unregulated market forces should determine economic outcomes—not the government. This requires that government not regulate any activity that encroaches on the ability of persons to enter into voluntary exchanges that are mutually acceptable to the parties to the bargain.

For example, it only took 1 year and 45 days for contractors to build the Empire State Building from its March 17, 1930 starting date. However, it took

Georgia 14 years to complete a $1 billion infrastructure project largely because of environmental and regulatory hurdles. Regardless of one's political affiliation, it certainly appears that, in some instances, government regulation may be objectively excessive. And, while government regulation isn't intrinsically inefficient, it has occasionally created inefficiencies in the American economy.

But the discussion of regulation tends to be much more complex. For example, artificial intelligence (AI) has the ability to improve life dramatically. However, there is now considerable research suggesting the ability of AI to destroy humanity. Nevertheless, some experts in the industry predict that no meaningful regulation will likely occur because of the money to be made by those with the ability to control the technology. Accordingly, regulation may only be forthcoming after a series of well-documented catastrophes occur. This is what normally must occur before regulation of business takes place in America.

Experts have said that some AI programs are currently sentient—i.e., AI currently can perceive and feel things. This includes emergent properties to be creative, to reason, and to plan; and the capability of thinking for themselves as humans. Accordingly, leading experts now say that there is every reason to believe that AI will be able to take control of itself. Geoffrey Hinton, known as the godfather of AI, says that smarter-than-human AI could be here in 5 to 20 years, compared with earlier estimates of 30 to 100 years.

Current risks include, among others, unleashing bots trained on racist and sexist information gathered from the web and distributing it in a manner that reinforces those ideas; making up false information and passing it off as factual; increasing social inequities; making the Internet even more skewed away from languages and cultures of most of humanity (because the majority of AI data training is done in English, North America, or Europe); disrupting high paying professions like law and medicine; creating copyright chaos; creating gaping holes in digital privacy and surveillance; and allowing governments to deploy deadly weapons that can kill without human control.

Nevertheless, for all of the reasons we have previously discussed, it is unlikely that the government will enact any substantial regulations until a series of calamities occur that demand political action to protect society. We discuss AI later in this book.

In the United States, the government has only enacted major economic and social welfare legislation as a matter of last resort. This is due, in part, to Americans' traditional suspicion of centralized power and authority. Thus, government regulation in the U.S. tends to be reactive and rarely proactive.

Examples of crises in America that have produced major legislation include the Civil War, the rise of business monopolies in the latter part of the 1800s, the bank panic of 1907 (which eventually led the U.S. to establish the Federal Reserve System), the collapse of the stock markets in 1929, the Great Depression of the 1930s, World War I, World War II, the Civil Rights Movement of the 1950s and 1960s, the collapse of Enron Corporation, the Great Recession of 2008, and the Covid-19 Recession of 2020 (aka the Great Lockdown).

In any event, one need not take a normative stance on the ethics of those who use a liberty-based defense to recognize the defense for how it is often used—*as a means to avoid liability for harming others.*

Accordingly, those who have used or may use liberty-based defenses to justify acts that harm others should not feel demeaned. Indeed, the U.S. Constitution's protections of freedom and liberty have proved to be "notoriously contested concept[s] as [their] meaning continuously shifts in different historical moments."[2]

A good illustration of the contested nature of what freedom means can be currently seen in the contrasting views of Florida governor Ron DeSantis and the editorial board of the *Washington Post*. On one hand, Florida governor Ron DeSantis refers to Florida as "a citadel of freedom," "freedom's linchpin," "freedom's vanguard," and "on the front lines of freedom." The editors of the *Washington Post*, however, see DeSantis' policies as a direct attack on freedom in Florida. In the *Post's* view, "Mr. DeSantis is waging frontal assaults on press freedom, reproductive freedom, free enterprise and academic freedom."

The *Post's* editors do not stop there. They also maintain that DeSantis, "in the name of protecting gun rights, has scaled back prudent safety rules"

---

2 ANKER, *supra* note 1 at 2.

and is "now poised to target undocumented immigrants, including 'dreamers,' with what will be some of the cruelest policies in America."

An even more striking illustration of the contested nature of freedom can be seen in the Southern Poverty Law Center's June 2023 declaration that an organization called **Moms for Liberty** can be correctly labeled as an "extremist group" devoted to spreading "messages of anti-inclusion and hate," "conspiracy theories" and "actions to censor school discussions around race, discrimination, and LGBTQ+ identities."

## A. Organizations That Provide Liberty-Based Defenses When Their Client's Actions Harm Others

Some organizations, such as the Alliance Defending Freedom, exist primarily to represent defendants who claim liberty-based justifications for violating the rights of others. The bottom line is that defendants who are successful in their liberty-based defenses avoid liability to persons who otherwise would have had legal recourse against these defendants for their injuries.[3]

For example, in 2023, The Alliance Defending Freedom, represented a website designer in the United States Supreme Court who sought to justify her refusal to provide services to a same-sex couple as required by a Colorado accommodations statute on the basis of the liberty provided by the Constitution's guarantee of freedom of speech.[4]

The website designer also claimed a liberty interest under the freedom of religion clauses to deny the same-sex couple services. However, the Court only agreed to hear the question of whether the application of the Colorado

---

3 Robert Barnes, *Justices Hold Testy Debate on Free Speech: Designer Who Wants to Refuse Same-Sex Clients Seems to Win Sympathy,* WASH. POST, December 6, 2022, at A1 (mentioning the role of the Alliance Defending Freedom's representation of the website designer), Wedding websites are the latest gay rights battleground in ...Washington Post https://www.washingtonpost.com › 2022/12/04 › colo...

4 *Id. See* 303 Creative LLC v. Elenis, 6 F. 4th 1160 (10th Cir. 2021), *cert. granted,* ___U.S.___ (February 22, 2022).

law would compel an artist to speak or stay silent in violation of the Free Speech Clause of the First Amendment.[5]

While the Court declined to hear the website designer's freedom of religion defense, individuals and entities have been flooding the U.S. courts with cases that maintain that "their right to religious freedom entitles them to refuse to comply with anti-discrimination laws."[6] The ultimate outcome of the website designer's case is not the point of this discussion. Rather, the focus, for purposes of this book, is on how persons often use freedom and liberty as justifications to avoid liability for harming others. *However, it is noteworthy* that, on June 30, 2023, the U.S. Supreme Court ruled that the website designer could avoid liability under the Colorado discrimination statute based on the U.S. Constitution's grant of the right to freedom of speech.

The Alliance Defending Freedom has also initiated lawsuits on behalf of conservative antiabortion plaintiffs who have challenged the federal government's authority to regulate abortion. Ironically, the Alliance has instituted these lawsuits only when the federal government appears to be advancing the liberty of women who choose to terminate a pregnancy.

For example, on November 18, 2022, the Alliance filed a lawsuit in which it contends: (1) that the FDA lacked authority to approve the abortion medication mifepristone—which the FDA approved decades ago; (2) that the FDA did not adequately study the medication; and (3) that the medication

---

5 *Id.* The Supreme Court declined to hear the website designer's claim that the Colorado law violated her religious freedom. Nor did it agree to hear the website designer's arguments that it should overturn Supreme Court precedent on neutral laws that might have implications for religious believers. One narrow subsidiary question before the Court was whether it should classify the website designer as an artist who would, then, have a First Amendment free speech right. The website designer's brief conceded that "hairstylists, landscapers, plumbers, caterers, tailors, jewelers and restaurants ordinarily wouldn't have a First Amendment free speech right to decline to serve a same-sex wedding."

6 Louise Melling, *Religion is no Excuse to Discriminate*, WASH. POST, September 8, 2022, When did religious belief become an excuse to discriminate? Washington Post https://www.washingtonpost.com › 2022/09/07 › supr...

is unsafe.[7] This is yet one more illustration of the clash between the desire of persons to be free of government regulation—at least when it is contrary to their ideological beliefs—versus the role of government to protect society generally and, occasionally, certain vulnerable segments of society. It is also an example of how persons use freedom and liberty-based arguments to limit or destroy the liberty rights of others, such as women who wish to terminate a pregnancy.

## B. Political Ideologies of Freedom That May be Harming Constituents

This book highlights many other ironies inherent in the concepts of freedom and liberty. Indeed, two alarming studies published in 2022 determined that many Americans are dying unnecessarily because of their political leaders' insistence that they be free from government regulations and programs designed to protect them. Both reports concluded that Americans who live in more conservative areas do not live as long as those in liberal or moderate jurisdictions.[8] Speaking to this issue, one political scientist noted that "[a]

---

7  Laura McGinley, Ariana Eunjung Cha, *Conservative Group Sues FDA in Bid to Revoke Approval of Abortion Pill*, November 19, 2022, at A4,
Conservative group sues FDA to revoke approval of . . . Washington Post https://www. washingtonpost.com › abortion-pill-lawsuit. We shall discuss the irony of the Supreme Court's decision to give states the freedom to ban a woman's liberty to terminate a pregnancy in this Introduction. However, we shall primarily address the Supreme Court's decision in Part II of this article. The name of the Supreme Court decision in question is *Dobbs v. Jackson Women's Health Organization*, 597 U.S. __, 142 S.Ct. 2228, (2022).

8  Akilah Johnson, *Studies Find Partisan Politics Can Affect People's Well-Being: Researchers Find Americans in More Conservative Areas Don't Live as Long*, WASH. POST, December 20, 2022, at A1, Can politics kill you? Research says the answer . . . Washington Post https://www.washingtonpost.com › health › 2022/12/16
In the December 22, 2022 study, The Harvard T. H. Chan School of Public Health performed a study that examined the health and longevity outcomes in each of the 435 congressional districts as well as state legislatures. In the other study, two University of Washington professors published a study, in October 2022, that found that conservative leaning jurisdictions could have avoided the deaths of hundreds of thousands of their citizens if they had implemented policies enacted by liberal jurisdictions in the areas of abortion, the environment, gun safety, criminal justice, health and welfare, and economic and tobacco taxes.

sense of liberty informed by a fatalistic acceptance that hardships happen in life is bedrock in many conservative areas." Accordingly, "[i]f liberty means you've got guns and that gun is accessible when you're having a depressive episode, they're not there to coddle other citizens. . . ."[9]

If the findings of these reports survive scrutiny, they will constitute one more example in which *partisan politics, based on liberty-based justifications to be free from government regulation, result in bad outcomes for people.*

The studies indicate that persons who reside in conservative congressional districts—characterized by leaders who champion small government, freedom from mask requirements, freedom from federal programs that support social welfare programs, freedom from federal health and welfare initiatives, and freedom from regulations involving the environment and gun safety, while also seeking to ban abortions—have significantly higher mortality rates than persons who live in jurisdictions that take the opposite approach.[10] Therefore, it is entirely consistent that the most conservative group in Congress refers to itself as the "Freedom Caucus."[11]

Let's take a quick look at the studies. One study, published by the Harvard T.H. Chan School of Public Health in December 2022, found that the more conservative the voting records of members of Congress and state legislators, the higher the age adjusted covid mortality rates. Moreover, the study affirmed these findings after taking into consideration the racial, education, and income characteristics of each of the 435 congressional districts examined. The study also found that, with respect to state legislatures, covid death rates were 11 percent higher in states with Republican-controlled governments and 26 percent higher in areas in which voters lean conservative.[12]

In the other study, two University of Washington professors published a study in October, 2022, that found that conservative leaning jurisdictions

---

9 *Id.* Comments of Erin O'Brien, a political scientist at the University of Massachusetts at Boston.

10 *Id.*

11 W. SHERMAN ROGERS, WINNERS AND LOSERS IN THE AMERICAN CAPITALISTIC ECONOMY: A PRIMER 8 (2016).

12 Akilah Johnson, *supra* note 8.

could have avoided the deaths of 170,000 of their citizens if they had implemented policies enacted by liberal jurisdictions in the areas of abortion, the environment, gun safety, criminal justice, health and welfare, economic and tobacco taxes. On the other hand, the report noted that if more liberal states had adopted the conservative, liberty-based variations of those policies, "there would have been about 217,000 more deaths that year—'the equivalent of a 600-passenger airplane crashing every day of the year.'"[13]

The report of the two University of Washington professors also found that "the largest projected number of lives saved—about 201,000—came from a more mixed menu of ideologies, with conservative marijuana policies and liberal polices on everything else."[14]

As Fareed Zakaria noted, the real story might be that people see their own interests in much more emotional and tribal ways than scholars understand. Zakaria openly wondered whether, in the eyes of a large group of Americans, issues involving religion, race, and culture are the ones for which people will stand up, protest, support politicians, and even pay an economic price.

## C. Some of the Ironies of Freedom

Interestingly, the research of epidemiologists Richard Wilson and Kate Pickett indicate, among other things, that countries like the U.S., that spend less of their national income on social services had greater rates of teen pregnancy, infant mortality, mental illness, drug use, imprisonment, and homicide than countries where wealth is more evenly distributed.[15]

At this point in our discussion, it should not be entirely surprising that the grand notions of freedom so prevalent in American law, politics, economics, and history often ignore the appalling violence that traffics under the banner of freedom. Therefore, it should not be shocking to many persons that the foundational philosophies of freedom set forth by John Locke, John Stuart

---

13 *Id.*

14 *Id.*

15 ROGERS, *supra* note 11, at 320.

Mill, and Immanuel Kant, "combine visions of emancipation from unjust authority with justification of despotism and inequality for 'uncivilized' nonwhite peoples. . . ."[16]

There is no higher value in American politics than freedom.[17] The Declaration of Independence and the Constitution of the United States sought, respectively, to set forth the ideal of liberty and to protect the country's inhabitants from specifically identified government intrusions on their liberty.

Consistent with these notions of liberty, the dominant political and economic thought in the U.S. until the 1930s—the classical school of economics (sometimes referred to as classical liberalism)—defined liberty to mean individual freedom from government interference and regulation, and the ability to organize relationships on the basis of free contracts between consenting adults. Classical liberals argued that individual freedom is more important than the welfare of society as a group.[18]

However, in the 1930s, Keynesian Economics[19] ended the dominance of classical economics in America. Nevertheless, Friedrich Hayek and Milton Friedman led a revival of interest in classical liberalism in the 20th century. Commentators refer to this movement as "neoclassical liberalism."[20]

Like its predecessor, neoliberalism depicts government as the primary source of unfreedom. But, ironically, as political scientist Elisabeth Anker notes, neoliberalism "also intensifies state power over the most insecure and marginalized segments of society." Indeed, "[s]urveillance and state violence have become essential aspects of the neoliberal management of escalating social and economic insecurity produced by decimated social safety nets and deregulated profitmaking." Consequently, the government has strengthened "carceral and securitized power over a growing number of people excluded from capital flows."[21]

---

16 ANKER, *supra* note 1, at 89.

17 *Id.* at 2.

18 ROGERS, *supra* note 11, at 17–18, 199–200.

19 *Id.* at 203, 314–315.

20 *Id.* at 199.

21 *Id.* at 199. See also ANKER, *supra* note 1, at 114.

Some scholars note that the United States and its most powerful elites—from colonial times to the present—have often used the word "freedom" to support a wide variety of efforts to exclude and harm people.[22] The following are few examples that these scholars have cited to illustrate the irony and complexity that underly the meaning of freedom.

- "Political theorist and slaveholder John C. Calhoun . . . argued that slavery was necessary for freedom and a positive good." Specifically, Calhoun referred to the freedom of local control and citizens' self-rule (i.e., individual and political sovereignty) as a justification for slavery. Such notions of freedom included the freedom to own private property as it authorized White property owners to use the labor of Black human property largely as they decided. And, even more ironic, this version of freedom allowed enslavers the leisure to write treatises on liberty.[23]

- At the time of the Constitutional Convention in Philadelphia, the law gave only 2 percent of the population the freedom to vote.[24]

- The freedom of the White master extended to torture, rape, and lifelong control over the humans he or she owned.[25]

- Twentieth century courts justified racial segregation as the freedom of White people to control human spaces.[26]

---

22 ANKER, *supra* note 1. *See also* Elizabeth Anker, *The Exploitation of "Freedom,"* NY Times, February 6, 2022, at 6 of Sunday Review.

23 ANKER, *supra* note 1, at 4.

24 Elizabeth Anker, *The Exploitation of "Freedom,"* N.Y. Times, February 6, 2022, at 6 of Sunday Review, Opinion | Freedom Is a Bad Defense for Ugly Behavior The New York Times
https://www.nytimes.com › 2022/02/04 › opinion › ugly . . .

25 *Id.*

26 *Id.*

- Governor George Wallace of Alabama grounded his position against integration as "our fight for freedom" and justified it as "the ideology of our free fathers."[27]

- In early American history, a man's freedom permitted domestic violence against his wife.[28]

- The pursuit of freedom has legitimated the forceful taking of land possessed by indigenous people, environmental destruction, sex and gender oppression, and a free market that allows the powerful few to accumulate vast wealth amid poverty and homelessness.[29]

- Significantly, the United States Supreme Court recently stripped women of their nearly 50-year-old liberty-based constitutional right to decide whether to terminate a pregnancy, in part, on the Tenth Amendment sovereign rights of states to decide the matter *for women* in the absence of a constitutional amendment or, perhaps, congressional legislation.[30]

---

27 *Id.*

28 *Id.*

29 ANKER, *supra* note 1, at 4.

30 *Dobbs v. Jackson Women's Health Organization*, 597 U.S. __, 142 S.Ct. 2228, (2022). The Court held that the legislatures of the states had the right to determine for women whether women residing in a particular state should be allowed to terminate a pregnancy and under what circumstances, if any. Accordingly, the Court held that the sovereign rights of state legislatures to ban abortion outweighed the liberty of a woman to choose to terminate a pregnancy. *Id.* at 2277, 2284.

Congress must have a sufficient Constitutional basis to enact legislation that would override a State's Tenth Amendment Authority to pass laws that ban abortion. This is because the United States Constitution has established a system of dual sovereignty between states and the federal government. The typical grounds for federal legislation of this nature would be the Commerce Clause, the Spending Clause, and Section 5 of the Fourteenth Amendment. The discussion of congressional authority to ban abortion is beyond the scope of this article. However, the Congressional Research Service has written a fairly good paper on this topic. *See generally,* Congressional Authority to Regulate Abortion—CRS Reportshttps://crsreports.congress.gov › LSB › LSB10787.

Accordingly, practices of freedom have often included enslavement; exploitation; the unfettered right to cause harm to others on the grounds of individual autonomy and sovereignty; and taking away the freedom of others in the name of individual or state sovereignty. These iterations of freedom have been as prominent as notions of freedom based on independence, emancipation, and democratic revolution. As W.E.B. Du Bois stated:

> Most men today cannot conceive of a freedom that does not involve somebody's slavery. They do not want equality because the thrill of their happiness comes from having things that others have not.[31]

Scholars and commentators have long praised the United States as an exceptional nation. They ground the doctrine of American exceptionalism on the fact that the United States is the only country in the world to have come into existence based on a creed of "liberty, egalitarianism, individualism, populism, and laissez faire." But again there are numerous ironies, some of which we have already mentioned, that significantly tarnish the concept.[32]

Judeo-Christian scriptures depict the first liberty-based movement as Lucifer's rebellion against God's government. There was a war in heaven, Lucifer lost the war, and God's government expelled Lucifer from heaven. Thereafter, at some point, Lucifer (aka Satan) persuaded Eve on planet Earth that liberty was better than following God's rules. Eve's choice did not turn out so well in the long run. However, it is clear that both Lucifer and Eve had the freedom to choose to disobey the established rules.[33]

Indeed, Judeo-Christian scriptures clearly place freedom of choice—as witnessed by God placing the tree of knowledge of good and evil in the middle of the garden—as one of the central themes of the creation.[34] Theologians

---

31  ANKER, *supra* note 1, at 37, quoting from Du Bois' book DARKWATER.

32  ROGERS, *supra* note 11, at 82.

33  Revelation 12:7.

34  Genesis 2:9.

and commentators, however, have debated whether freedom of choice and liberty can coexist in a theoretical heaven in which certain rules of behavior must be followed. This debate is exemplified by some antiabortion advocates who implicitly fault God in placing the tree of knowledge of good and evil in the garden of Eden. In their view, God should have prohibited humans from having a choice to disobey God's laws and prohibitions. Therefore, they feel empowered to strip women of their previous liberty to choose whether to terminate a pregnancy.[35]

The same debate over freedom of choice exists with respect to life on Earth. Indeed, this seems to be the underlying theme of **the dystopian**[36] **drama film *The Giver*,** directed by Phillip Noyce and starring Jeff Bridges, Brenton Thwaites, Odeya Rush, Meryl Streep, Alexander Skarsgard, Katie Holmes, Camereon Monoghan, Taylor Swift, and Emma Tremblay. We shall discuss this subject and the movie in Part II of this book, which serves as the book's Background section.

Scholars have traditionally considered a person's freedom to engage in certain protected conduct, free of government encroachment, as the goal of liberty. The American notion of liberty, as enshrined in the U.S. Constitution,[37] is in stark contrast to the authoritarian regimes found in some countries. For

---

35 Wesley Knight, Sermon titled, "The Choice is Yours—A Word on Abortion," You Tube (May 21,2022).

36 A dystopia is a fictional community or society that is undesirable or frightening. Dystopias are often characterized by rampant fear, distress, tyrannical governments, environmental disaster, and other characteristics associated with a cataclysmic decline in society. Commentators often use the term as an antonym of utopia, a term created by Sir Thomas More which served as the title of his best-known work which More published in 1516. Utopia created a blueprint for an ideal society with minimal crime, violence, and poverty. *See Dystopias: Definition and Characteristics,* Read Write Think (2006) (PDF); Definition of dystopia, Merriam-Webster Dictionary. Merriam-Webster, Inc. 2012.

37 Those freedoms include freedom of religion, freedom of speech, freedom of the press, freedom of assembly, the right to bear arms, the freedom from unreasonable searches and seizures, the freedom against self-incrimination, the right to be free of any government taking of a person's private property without just compensation, the right to be free from cruel and unusual punishment, and the right of persons to be free from any government deprivation of a person's life, liberty, or property, without due process, and even the rights of states to be free from some aspects of domination by the U.S. federal government. Part II, which serves as the Background section of this article, provides slightly more detail on these constitutional provisions.

example, during the summer of 2021, government suppression of liberty were on vivid display in the countries of Myanmar, Cuba, Nicaragua, and Belarus. And, notably, China passed an array of regulations that made deep intrusions over its people's rights of speech and expression.

Traditionally, these types of government encroachments on personal liberty have been the concern of persons in the United States. Indeed, during the so-called *Lochner* era, the United States Supreme Court, relying on a theory of natural rights and the Due Process Clauses of the Fifth and Fourteenth Amendments, routinely struck down state and federal laws if the Court believed that these laws interfered with the property rights of persons and the rights of persons to freely enter into contracts without government interference.[38]

Interestingly, the government often intended to protect the most vulnerable persons in society when it enacted these laws that the Court struck down in the name of liberty. However, the court considered the property interests of business owners and their liberty to freely enter into bilateral contracts more important.[39]

However, there is a segment of the U.S. population that believes that the concept of liberty extends well beyond the freedom to be free of government intrusions explicitly set forth in the Constitution. Adherents of "pure capitalism," for example, believe that the only role of government is to protect its citizens and their property.[40] Therefore, they frown on any government regulation or government program that impinges on the ability of persons to use the resources they control to enter into bilateral, voluntary, and informed exchanges that are mutually acceptable to the parties to the bargain.[41]

In short, they believe that people should be free of all government rules, regulations, and programs that restrict the actions of people. The most extreme

---

38 ROGERS, *supra* note 11, at 99–100. This period of American History takes its name from the case of Lochner v. United States, 198 U.S. 45,45 (1905).
39 ROGERS, *supra* note 11, at 100.
40 *Id.* at 226.
41 *Id.*

version of this belief has been advocated by economists who describe themselves as "right-libertarian advocates of anarcho-capitalism."[42]

## D. Nineteen Examples Where Liberty-Based Arguments are Involved in Legal, Regulatory and Policy Decisions

### *Helmet Law Cases as an Example of Liberty-Based Arguments to be Free of Government Regulation*

Cases involving helmet laws serve as a great illustration of what is involved. For years , people have fought against helmet laws as violating their freedom to ride their bikes without a helmet. "It's all about freedom. Freedom of choice, freedom of expression, right to privacy, and now, freedom of religion." And, yet, it is undisputable that helmets save lives and economic costs.[43] On the other hand, if a bike rider suffers a preventable brain injury, the public at large eventually pays for his or her healthcare.[44]

There are countless other examples in which people (including private businesses) protest government regulation in favor of unfettered freedom of choice. This includes the right of persons to put themselves in harm's way in the name of freedom.

---

42 ROGERS, *supra* note 11, at 7–8, 12–13, 18–20, 54–57, *59–61*, 99–100, 107–112, 214–245. *See also*, Lizzie O'Leary, *The Anti-Krugman, The Anti-Krugman Libertarians at Sea*, Bloomberg Businessweek, September 30, 2019, at 48,
The Libertarians on the Anti-Krugman Cruise Just Want to . . . https://www.bloomberg.com › news › features › a-wee . . . (noting that some on the cruise identify as "AnCaps" or anarcho-capitalists," meaning they'd happily get rid of the state and let society self-regulate through the free market").

43 *See* Mandatory Helmet Laws—Freedom Or Safety Issue? EatSleepRIDE https://eatsleepride.com › mandatory_helmet_laws_-_f...

44 Melissa Neiman, *Motorcycle Helmet Laws: The Facts, What Can Be Done to Jump-Start Helmet Use, and Ways to Cap Damages,* 11 J. Health Care L & Pol'y 215 (2008), available at http://digitalcommons.law.umaryland.edu/jhclp/vol11/iss2/3; Anti-Helmet Issues—Bicycle Helmet Safety Institute
https://helmets.org › negativs; Mandatory Helmet Laws—Freedom Or Safety Issue? EatSleepRIDE https://eatsleepride.com › mandatory_helmet_laws_-_f...

Additionally, it appears that *courts and government officials often rely on political, ideological, and moral arguments to determine which people they will allow to exercise their liberty-based claims.* A clear example of this is the United States Supreme Court decision in *Dobbs v. Jackson Women's Health Organization.*[45]

### *Other Examples Where People and Entities Base Arguments to be Free of Government Regulation on Notions of Either Freedom, Liberty, Sovereignty and Neoliberalism*

The following are seventeen additional examples in which people and entities base arguments against government laws and regulations on notions of freedom and individual rights.

- Whether the government should be able to dictate that people wear masks and take vaccines during the global pandemic?

- Whether all laws prohibiting discrimination should be abolished?

- Whether the government should regulate the contamination of the environment or wildlife conservation?

---

45  597 U.S. __, 142 S.Ct. 2228 (2022). The Court's majority opinion held that the Fourteenth Amendment's reference to "liberty" does not protect the right of a woman to have an abortion. In the Court's view, abortion is different from other rights based on a person's right to privacy and ability to make personal choices that are central to a person's dignity and autonomy. The Court noted that "none" of the Court's prior cases based on liberty rights "involved the critical moral question posed by abortion." Unlike the other liberty-based rights the Court protected in other cases, only abortion permitted the destruction of what *Roe* termed "potential life" and what the challenged Mississippi law referred to as the killing of an "unborn human being." *Id.* at 2257–2258. The Court stated that it was this critical moral question that made the issue of abortion "unique." *Id.* at 2277. For this reason, the Court held that the legislatures of the states had the right to determine for women whether women residing in a particular state should be allowed to terminate a pregnancy and under what circumstances, if any. Accordingly, the Court held that the sovereign rights of state legislatures outweighed the liberty of a woman to choose to terminate a pregnancy. *Id.* at 2277, 2284.

- Whether it was wise for the government to enact Social Security legislation?

- Whether it was wise for the government to pass antipoverty legislation?

- Whether it was wise for the government to enact any antitrust laws? And, if so, whether the antitrust laws should be used to thwart certain practices utilized by Facebook, Amazon, Google, and Microsoft?

- Whether it is wise for the government to enact rent control laws?

- Whether the government should have ever enacted minimum wage laws?

- Whether the government should support labor unions?

- Whether the government should enact safety rules to protect workers and consumers?

- Whether it is wise for the government to enact occupational licensing laws?

- Whether cryptocurrency should be regulated?

- Whether prohibitions against insider trading of securities should be abolished?

- Whether it is appropriate for the government to regulate the business model of Uber, Lyft, and other gig economy companies?

- Whether the government should regulate the development and use of artificial intelligence (face recognition, algorithms that create disparate racial effects, etc.)?

- Whether the GameStop stock trading mania in "meme" stocks was the inevitable result of decades of lax regulation?

- Whether the hard freeze in Texas in 2021 exposed the dangers of Texas' deregulated and independent electric power grid?

The list is potentially endless. However, the liberty of people and private firms to do as they please without any government command or control is the common thread that links each of these examples.

This book addresses each of these nineteen examples. The nineteen examples include the continuing controversy over State helmet laws. They also include a brief discussion of the Supreme Court's rationale for its decision to strip women of their liberty-based right to an abortion and to give authority over that decision to the States.

*The goal in discussing these examples is not to provide an in-depth analysis of these topics.* That is beyond the scope of this book. Indeed, you may not be particularly interested in the underlying subject matter of some of the examples. Rather, *the sole objective in exploring these nineteen examples is to illustrate how people and entities use notions of freedom, liberty, personal sovereignty, government sovereignty, and neoliberalism as grounds to be free of government regulation and/ or to suppress the liberty of others.*

Accordingly, this book will provide just enough information for the reader to, hopefully, be able to understand the subject matter involved in the examples for the ultimate purpose of illustrating the arguments advanced by some against government regulation of their actions in the context of these examples.

Underlying the discussion are the frequent clashes between the desire of persons to be free of government regulation versus the role of government to protect society generally and, occasionally, certain vulnerable segments of society.

## E. Differences Between Republicans and Democrats in Their Approach to Government Regulation

In the United States, the government has only enacted major economic and social welfare legislation as a matter of last resort. This is due, in part, to Americans' traditional suspicion of centralized power and authority. Thus, government regulation in the U.S. tends to be reactive and rarely proactive.

The Trump Administration's approach to government regulation—consistent with the general Republican party narrative—was that "regulation and economic activity are inversely related—that is, less regulation always means more economic growth." On the other hand, those who generally identify as Democrats view "smart" regulation of the economy as producing a net increase in economic productivity.[46] However, not all regulation is "smart." And, sometimes, regulation can be excessive, counterproductive, or unnecessary.

For example, in 1930, it took 1 year and 45 days for builders to erect the Empire State Building, the tallest building in the world at the time. However, it took Georgia 14 years to complete a $1 billion infrastructure project largely because of environmental and regulatory hurdles.[47]

These regulatory hurdles also make construction projects more expensive. For example, in order to build 1 kilometer of rail, it costs Japan $170 million, Canada $254 million, and Germany $278 million. On the other hand, it costs the United States $538 million. In other words, while government regulation isn't intrinsically inefficient, excessive regulation has occasionally created inefficiencies in the American economy.[48]

## F. The Clash Between Government Regulation and Freedom

A threshold question that we must address in this book is why people choose to have a government in the first place. In this context, government means "an environment in which one will not have free rein to exercise all of one's choices."[49]

---

46 Catherine Rampell, *How Regulation Can Be Pro-Market*, WASH. POST, September 11, 2020, at A19, Please regulate us, beg companies that Trump keeps ...Washington Post https://www.washingtonpost.com › 2020/09/10.

47 George F. Will, *Can America Do Big Things Again? Ask the Regulators*, WASH. POST, June 16, 2022, at A21, Can America 'do big things' again? Ask the regulators and . . . Marshall News Messenger https://www.marshallnewsmessenger.com › can-america- . . . ; About NYC's Most Famous Building | Empire State Building, https://www.esbnyc.com/about#:~:text=Construction%20was%20completed%20in%20a,1%20year%20and%2045%20days.&text=Beautiful%20inside%20and%20out%2C%20the,marvel%20beloved%20across%20the%20world.

48 *Id.*

49 *See* JEFFREY L. HARRISON, *supra* note 1, at 429, (5th Ed.).

The most common risk in any governmental arrangement is that one may find that he or she is part of a minority whose freedoms must be limited to satisfy or increase the utility of the majority. Supreme Court cases such as *Bowers v. Hardwick*,[50] *Korematsu v. United States*,[51] and *Plessy v. Ferguson*,[52] illustrate that in a utilitarian world, there will be losers as well as winners.[53]

Conservative economist Robert P. Murphy argues that when government intervenes in the capitalist free market system of supply and demand, "it not only tramples on freedom, and individual rights, but also often hurts the very people it presumes to help."[54]

Every government tax and spending program has some redistributive effect. Many government welfare programs, for instance, seem designed to help a relatively small group of people such as the poor. But other programs benefit the relatively rich.[55] Accordingly, in every government tax and spending program, there will be net beneficiaries of the program or net contributors.[56]

The concept of "economic efficiency" has two major competing factions— one which emphasizes distortions created by the government (and remedied by decreasing the role of government) and distortions caused by markets (and reduced by increasing government involvement).[57]

Most commonly, **economic efficiency** (*which considers ideas of equality and distributive justice as irrelevant in reaching its conclusions*) is **contrasted with government welfare economics** (*which involves trade-offs between efficiency and distributive justice*).[58]

It is inevitable that people will ultimately end up as either net contributors or net recipients in essentially every government distribution program. Thus, issues

---

50  478 U.S.186 (1986).

51  323 U.S. 214 (1944).

52  163 U.S. 537 (1896).

53  HARRISON, *supra* note 1, at 437.

54  ROGERS, *supra* note 11, at 216, citing to Robert P. Murphy.

55  HARRISON, *supra* note 1, at 444–445.

56  *Id.* at 437.

57  ROGERS, *supra* note 11, at 95.

58  *Id.* at 95–96.

of fairness—i.e., the government's use of its taxing powers to take a larger amount of money from one group of persons to give to another group of persons—underly much of the debate. Therefore, the goal of government welfare economics is to address issues of economic inequality and economic efficiency in such a manner that those who become better off as a result of a government policy or program only receive a benefit to the extent that those at the bottom of the distribution chain (in some instances, the more affluent) also are made better off.[59]

This book maintains that government should attempt to improve social safety net programs to provide for universal healthcare, housing, daycare, and greater subsidization for food. These goals are not hostile to notions of free market capitalism and freedom of choice.[60] Indeed, even neoliberal theorists have recognized that government intervention is warranted in the provision of public goods and services—i.e., where it would be exceedingly costly and inefficient for the private sector to provide certain goods and services.[61]

Also encompassed in this position is the notion that the government does not infringe on the freedom of entities and persons when it enacts targeted, smart, regulation of persons and entities sufficient to assure the health, safety, and general welfare of people in the least burdensome manner. Most government regulation concerns efforts to respond to externalities[62] and the reduction of transaction costs for consumers.[63] We discuss the subject of externalities in Part II and Part III of this book. However, the primary examination of the topic of externalities takes place in Part III.

## G. Possible Solutions

The thesis of this book is that a system of regulated capitalism operating under a government welfare economic approach to capitalism does not interfere with the freedom of persons or entities and is the best way to ensure a better future

---

59 *Id.* at 7–10.

60 ROGERS, *supra* note 11, at 121–127.

61 *Id,* at 30–31, 59–61, 101–102, 214–215.

62 ROGERS, *supra* note 11, at 64–68. HARRISON, *supra* note 1, at 328, 335.

63 HARRISON, *supra* note 1, at 328–335. *See also* at 77–103.

for all people. It is the system followed by all developed capitalistic nations in the West. Historically, however, countries associated with the European Union have been stronger adherents to the philosophy underlying government welfare economics than the United States.[64]

In Part II of this book, we shall provide greater background information and discussion of the matters raised in the Introduction.

In Part III, we shall provide a brief analysis—both pro and con—for and against regulation in the 19 areas we mentioned earlier. This book addresses each of these nineteen examples; not to provide an in-depth discussion of the topics but to illustrate how liberty-based arguments to be free of government regulation undergirds each claim.

Additionally, we shall briefly discuss the pros and cons of Donald Trump's efforts to: (1) rollback civil and human rights regulations in 395 instances; (2) weaken environmental protections in 74 deregulatory actions; (3) repeal the Patient Protection and Affordable Care Act (Obamacare); (4) deregulate the energy and financial sectors; and (5) respond to the Covid-19 Pandemic through a Tenth Amendment State sovereignty-based decentralized approach that emphasized personal liberty rights as being more important than the welfare of society as a group.

In Part IV, we shall discuss the ideal approach to government regulation.

Part V of this book consists of a brief conclusion. In the final analysis, this book concludes that a system of regulated capitalism operating under a government welfare economic approach is the best way to ensure a better future for all people. No nation in the 21st century has yet to adopt the libertarian utopian state of a bare-bones, minimalist government, and it is unlikely that any nation will.[65] Additionally, this book maintains that a government should base its decision to regulate on John Rawl's "a theory of justice."[66]

---

64 ROGERS, *supra* note 11, at 95–96.

65 *Id.* at 54.

66 HARRISON, *supra* note 1 at 438–439. "Central to the Rawlsian model is the belief that people are risk-averse." Indeed, "[t]hey are so risk-averse they adopt a decision-making rule called 'maximin.' Under a maximin rule, [people] assume they will ultimately be among the worst off in society and then choose the governing principles that would maximize the welfare of the worst off."

# PART II

# BACKGROUND

## A. American Exceptionalism: Liberty, Egalitarianism, and Individualism

*The Declaration of Independence* and the Constitution of the United States sought, respectively, to set forth the ideal of liberty and to legally protect the country's inhabitants from specifically identified government intrusions on their liberty. Accordingly, the Declaration of Independence sets forth the ideals of universal equality and the right to life, liberty, and the pursuit of happiness. And the Constitution legally prohibits the government from intruding on several specified liberties granted to persons residing in the United States.

Those liberties include, among others, freedom of religion,[67] freedom of speech,[68] freedom of the press,[69] freedom of assembly,[70] the right to bear arms,[71] the freedom from unreasonable searches and seizures,[72] the freedom against self-incrimination,[73] the right to be free of any government taking of a person's private property without just compensation,[74] and the right of

---

67 U.S. CONST. amend. I.

68 *Id.*

69 *Id.*

70 *Id.*

71 U.S. CONST. amend. II.

72 U.S. CONST. amend. IV.

73 U.S. CONST. amend. V.

74 *Id.*

persons to be free from any government deprivation of a person's life, liberty, or property, without due process of law.[75]

Scholars and commentators base the doctrine of American exceptionalism on the fact that the United States is the only country in the world to have come into existence based on a creed of "liberty, egalitarianism, individualism, populism, and laissez faire."[76] The notion of American exceptionalism also embodies an ideological commitment to personal liberty, an anti-government doctrine that extols laissez faire economics, and rejects the idea of a government-established church.

As a doctrine, the concept of American exceptionalism also frowns on the idea that the government should ever recognize a class of aristocrats with landed estates to whom the government has bestowed titles based on hereditary nobility.

Indeed, the United States constitution explicitly prohibits the U.S. from granting titles of nobility (article I, section 9, clause 8) and from establishing an official government church (first amendment to the constitution).

In this sense, proponents of American exceptionalism contend that the United States is exceptional in that it was founded on a set of republican ideals rather than on a common heritage, ethnicity, or ruling elite.

## B. The First Liberty-Based Movement

Judeo-Christian scriptures depict the first liberty-based movement as Lucifer's rebellion against God's government. There was a war in heaven, Lucifer lost the war, and God's government expelled Lucifer from heaven. Thereafter, at some point, Lucifer (aka Satan) persuaded Eve on planet Earth that liberty was better than following God's rules. Eve's choice did not turn out so well in the long run. However, it is clear that both Lucifer and Eve had the freedom to choose to disobey the established rules.

---

75  U.S. CONST. amend. V and XIV.

76  ROGERS, *supra* note 11, at 82.

Theologians and commentators have debated whether freedom of choice and liberty can coexist in a theoretical heaven in which certain rules of behavior must be followed. The same debate exists with respect to life on Earth.

Thus, some antiabortion advocates implicitly fault God in placing the tree of knowledge of good and evil in the garden of Eden. In their view, God should have prohibited humans from having a choice to disobey God's laws and prohibitions. Therefore, they feel empowered to strip women of their previous liberty to choose whether to terminate a pregnancy.

This was the underlying theme of the dystopian drama film *The Giver*, directed by Phillip Noyce and starring Jeff Bridges, Brenton Thwaites, Odeya Rush, Meryl Streep, Alexander Skarsgard, Katie Holmes, Camereon Monoghan, Taylor Swift, and Emma Tremblay.[77]

The movie depicts a fictious country—apparently cut off from the rest of the world. The country requires its inhabitants to swallow a pill daily to control their emotions and the choices they make. The government's ostensible goal is to keep its residents from making bad choices. The movie seems to identify these bad choices as decisions based on pride, envy, lust, and passion. It is for this reason that the government requires its inhabitants to take the

---

77 *See Dystopias, supra* note 36. A dystopia is a fictional community or society that is undesirable or frightening. Dystopias are often characterized by rampant fear, distress, tyrannical governments, environmental disaster, and other characteristics associated with a cataclysmic decline in society. Some authors have used the term to refer to existing societies which are, typically, totalitarian states in an advanced state of collapse.

Dystopian fiction often focuses, among other things, on: (1) stark contrasts between the privileges of the ruling class and the dreary existence of the working class; (2) people who are at the mercy of a state-controlled economy run by plutocrats; (3) large corporations that have replaced government in setting policy and making decisions; (4) countries in which excessive pollution has destroyed nature; (5) technologies that reflect and encourage the worst aspects of human nature; and (5) religious-based theocratic regimes that impose their values on others.

Commentators often use the term as an antonym of utopia, a term created by Sir Thomas More which served as the title of his best-known work which More published in 1516. Utopia created a blueprint for an ideal society with minimal crime, violence, and poverty. *See Dystopias: Definition and Characteristics*, Read Write Think (2006) (PDF); Definition of dystopia, Merriam-Webster Dictionary. Merriam-Webster, Inc. 2012, *supra* note 36.

government-issued daily pill it distributes to extinguish these dangerous and undesirable impulses.

The subliminal message of the movie is that unfettered freedom of choice is the cause of the misery and suffering in the world. In the view of the country's leaders, freedom is a bad idea because when people are left to their own devices, they make bad choices. *Conflict, pain, and suffering have been mostly removed from the community. But love, freedom, individuality, and joy have also been removed.*[78]

It is for this reason that the country's leaders have caused babies to be brought into the world through genetic engineering and have suppressed its inhabitants' sexual desire through the government-issued daily pill. All memories of the past are held by one person—the Receiver of Memory—to shield the rest of society from pain. This person is known as the Giver.

Indeed, the country had once experienced despair, crime, suffering, poverty, and misery in the past. The country's inhabitants do not appear to know of this past. They seem to be mere automatons devoid of any spontaneous passion and desire.[79]

The movie indicates that the travails and suffering of humanity have continued to exist in other parts of the world. However, in this controlled country, everyone obeys the rules and appears to be passive, robotic followers of the country's rules of behavior. Only the Giver, government officials, and certain others have the capacity to make free choices, to be consciously aware of the country's past, and to have the ability to know evil as well as good. This is a continuation of the debate whether freedom of choice and liberty can exist even in a theoretical heaven if God forces everyone to follow the rules.[80]

---

78 Plot Summary (5)—The Giver (2014)—IMDb https://www.imdb.com › title › plotsummary.
79 *Id.*
80 *Id. See also* Wesley Knight, Sermon titled, "The Choice is Yours—a Word on Abortion," YouTube (May 21, 2022).

## C. The Libertarian Utopian State of Bare-Bones Minimalist Government

Libertarianism is at the core of the belief system that guides the new generation of politicians in America. Libertarians maintain that any government activity that extends beyond the protection of people from violence, theft, or enforcing contracts is illegitimate. Consequently, they *support* all efforts to *reduce* government programs such as public schools, Medicare, environmental regulation, and food stamps. And for consistency purposes, they *oppose* any legislation that *increases* government activity such as the Patient Protection and Affordable Care Act (the short name for which is simply the Affordable Care Act).[81]

Libertarianism is a type of *anti-statism*—a term that describes opposition to government intervention (i.e., intervention by "the state") into personal, social and economic affairs. "Anti-statists views may reject the state completely as well as rulership in general (e.g., anarchism)," or they may reflect a desire "to reduce the size and scope of the state to a minimum (e.g., minarchism), or they may advocate a stateless society as a distant goal."[82]

*Overall, libertarians believe that America should be governed by individual liberty, a peaceful foreign policy, minimal government* (limited to protecting people from violence, theft, and enforcing contracts), *and a free market economy.* They are of the view that any government activity beyond this is illegitimate. As one commentator observed, "Libertarians . . . seem to have persuaded themselves that there is no significant trade-off between less government and more national insecurity, more crime, more illiteracy and more infant and maternal mortality. . . ."[83]

No country has ever utilized a purely libertarian form of government. In the United States, however, America did have a government that, at least minimally, resembled the libertarian ideal in the late 19th century (i.e., the

---

81 ROGERS, *supra* note 11, at 54.

82 *Id.*

83 *Id.* at 55.

late 1800s). Indeed, during this period in American history, America had an economic system that operated much like the small-government model that libertarians champion. However, Americans decided that it did not work and rejected the libertarian ideal of a severely restricted role for government in the affairs of its people. Why was this the case? E.J. Dionne, Jr., a columnist for the *Washington Post*, provided what he believed to be the answer to this question in a June 10, 2013 article titled "It's Called Utopian for a Reason."[84] In the article, Mr. Dionne states that in America:

> We realized that many Americans would never be able to save enough for retirement and, later, that most of them would be unable to afford health insurance when they were old. Smaller government meant that too many people were poor and that monopolies were formed too easily.
>
> And when the Great Depression engulfed us, government was helpless, largely handcuffed by this anti-government ideology until Franklin D. Roosevelt came along.[85]

Would the United States be better off as a nation if there were essentially no government sponsored safety-net programs, no central bank, and virtually no regulation of business activity? That is a question that only each American can answer through the political process.

## D. The Libertarian-Tinged Antiregulatory Approach During the Lochner Era

The breakneck speed of economic development of the United States as a new nation coincided with the rise of laissez-faire economic theory. Many English and American philosophers during the early days of the nation adhered to the "natural rights" theory which held that certain rights—especially the right to

---

84 *Id.* at 56.
85 *Id.* at 56–57.

own property and the right to contract freely—were fundamental or natural rights which existed independently of any legal enactment.[86]

The U.S. Supreme Court subsequently came to view the ratification of the Fourteenth Amendment to the United States Constitution in 1868 as the link which empowered the Court to engage in a substantive review of state laws which encroached on property rights and the right of persons to freely enter into contracts. This was because of the Fourteenth Amendment's explicit prohibition of any state action which deprives a person of liberty and property without due process of law. Accordingly, the Court felt empowered to strike down laws that it believed to constitute an unwarranted interference with a person's right to freely make economic decisions. The Court also engaged in a similar review of federal legislation under the Due Process Clause of the Fifth Amendment to the United States Constitution.[87]

During the *Lochner* era of American legal history, a majority of the members on the U.S. Supreme Court officially adopted the views of both Adam Smith and Herbert Spencer in many of its decisions. Between 1897 and 1937, the Court struck down approximately 197 state and federal laws designed to protect the most vulnerable in society—e.g., minimum wage legislation and federal regulation of child labor—on the grounds that these laws abridged the economic liberty of business firms to enter into contracts protected by the Due Process Clause of the U.S. Constitution.

This period in American history takes its name from the case of *Lochner v. United States*.[88] In *Lochner*, the Court invalidated a New York law which limited the number of hours a bakery employee could work to no more than 10 hours per day and no more than 60 hours per week. According to the Court, the New York law which restricted the number of hours an employee could work abridged the right of the bakery owner to enter into contracts agreed on by the parties in violation of the Due Process Clause of the Fourteenth Amendment. In dissent, Justice Oliver Wendell Holmes lambasted the major-

---

86 *Id.* at 99.

87 *Id.*

88 198 U.S. 45 (1905).

ity's opinion noting that the Fourteenth Amendment "does not enact Mr. Herbert Spencer's social statics."[89]

Implicit in many of the Court's decisions during this era of American history was the notion that the government could not permissibly impose laws upon individuals and corporations that sought to redistribute economic and social power by taking property from one person to give to another. The Court majority generally viewed the misery of the underprivileged and the poor as an "inescapable corollary of personal freedom" and "an inevitable result of forces beyond human control."[90]

The economic realities of the great depression of the 1930s played the greatest role in the demise of the *Lochner* era. The depression undermined Adam Smith's invisible hand theory—a theory that maintained that the only proper way to protect individual rights and to produce the optimum level of economic productivity for all members of society, is for the government to allow the marketplace to exclusively determine the economic affairs of people.

Beginning in 1937, the Supreme Court, succumbing to pressure from every corner, ceased to impose its laissez-faire views of what it considered to be correct economic policy on legislative bodies. Today, in contrast, the Court engages in a presumption that a legislative provision designed to advance the health, safety and welfare of people is constitutional unless there is no rational basis to support the government regulation.[91]

## E. Traditional Goals of Liberty

Scholars have traditionally considered a person's freedom to engage in certain protected conduct, free of government encroachment, as the goal of liberty. Scholars and commentators once considered these types of blatant government deprivations of freedom as the *primary goal* of liberty. Real world examples of government suppression of the liberty of its people were on vivid display

---

89 ROGERS, *supra* note 11, at 99–100.
90 *Id.* at 100.
91 *Id.*

during the summer of 2021 in the countries of Myanmar, Cuba, Nicaragua, and Belarus.

During the summer of 2021, "dictators" [in those countries] . . . aggressively destroy[ed] the [institutions]" that are central to any "open and free society[s]" ability to function. Those institutions and instrumentalities most often subject to government suppression include: "news media, unions, political parties, movements and their leaders." A *Washington Post* editorial, reporting on these worldwide assaults to free society, stated: "Welcome to the summer of freedom lost."[92]

China's authoritarian control over its people during the summer of 2021 was particularly noteworthy. For example, Chinese authorities banned, "American Idol-style competitions and shows featuring men deemed too effeminate." Additionally, China scrubbed from the Internet any news mentions of one of its wealthiest actresses, Zhao Wei, including her movies and television series as if she had never existed.[93]

China's actions were part of "[a] dizzying regulatory crackdown unleashed by China's government [that] . . . spared almost no sector over the past few months" during the summer of 2021. The crackdowns included regulations that: (1) banned for-profit tutoring, an act that decimated China's multibillion-dollar private education sector; (2) dictated the amount of time children can spend playing video games; (3) required that broadcasters encourage masculinity and put a stop to showing "sissy men"; (4) required the elimination of content promoting "incorrect values" such as "money worship"; (5)"ban[ned] karaoke songs deemed out of line with the 'core values of socialism'"; and (6) regulated dancing in China's parks, which is a popular pastime for retirees.[94]

Rana Mitter, a professor of Modern Chinese history and politics at the University of Oxford, stated that the Chinese government "does not feel

---

92 See *Democracy in Distress: With Free Society Under Attack Worldwide, It's Time to Think Beyond Sanctions and Scolding,* Washington Post Editorial, August 29, 2021, A24.

93 Lily Kuo, *In Xi's Crackdown, a Remake of Chinese Society,* Washington Post, September 10, 2021, A1, Xi Jinping's crackdown on everything is remaking Chinese …Washington Post https://www.washingtonpost.com › world › 2021/09/.

94 *Id.*

comfortable with expressions of individualism that are in some ways transgressive to norms that it puts forward." Consequently, "the party-state makes it clear that it has the first and last word on what is permitted in mass culture." However, one Chinese student noted that China's regulatory measures may have gone too far. The student noted: "There is a point where government regulations stop working. You can ban artists and certain movies or songs, but you cannot teach people what to think."[95]

## F. The Antigovernment/Antiregulatory Movement in the United States

There is a segment of the U.S. population that believes that the notion of liberty extends well beyond the liberty to be free of government intrusions explicitly set forth in the Constitution. These adherents of "pure capitalism" believe that the only role of government is to protect its citizens and their property.[96] They frown on any government regulation or government program that impinges on the ability of persons to use the resources they control to enter into bilateral, voluntary, and informed exchanges that are mutually acceptable to the parties to the bargain.[97]

Consequently, they believe that people should be free of all government rules, regulations, and programs that restrict the actions of people. The most extreme version of this belief has been advocated by economists who describe themselves as "right-libertarian advocates of anarcho-capitalism."[98]

For years, people have fought against helmet laws as violating their freedom to ride their bikes without a helmet. On the other hand, if the bike riders suffer a preventable brain injury, the public at large eventually pays for

---

95 *Id.*

96 ROGERS, *supra* note 11, at 226.

97 *Id.*

98 ROGERS, *supra* note 11, at 7–8, 12–13, 18–20, 54–57, *59–61*, 99–100, 107–112, 214–245; Lizzie O'Leary, *The Anti-Krugman, The Anti-Krugman Libertarians at Sea, supra* note 42 (noting that some on the cruise identify as "AnCaps" or "anarcho-capitalists," meaning they'd happily get rid of the state and let society self-regulate through the free market").

their healthcare. There are countless other examples in which people (including private businesses) protest goverment regulation in favor of unfettered freedom of choice.

Indeed, during the deadliest moments of the global pandemic, some people consistently refused to abide by **mask mandates** or to get potentially life-saving vaccinations. Some refused to take these potentially life-saving precautions solely in the name of liberty and freedom of choice. It apparently made no difference that the Centers for Disease Control and Prevention and experts armed with studies continued to state that the failure to wear a mask could potentially cause massive outbreaks of the coronavirus.

One example of this involved an unvaccinated California teacher who was temporarily unmasked. The incident highlighted the potential danger for children under the age of 12—the only group in the United States ineligible for coronavirus vaccines at the time.[99] Yet, governments in some jurisdictions continued to actively oppose both mask and vaccine requirements even as the hyper-infectious delta variant sped across the country. Thus, it is clear that people often put themselves in harms way in the name of freedom.

People who do not get vaccinated pose a threat to the population at large (e.g., measles and other highly communicable diseases). On the other hand, people who get vaccinated produce what economists refer to as a positive consumption externality. This is because these consumers *"decrease the chances that others will become infected."*[100]

Nevertheless, some commentators and scholars view *government safety mandates as rules that trample on freedom and individual rights.*[101]

---

99 Ariana Eunjung Cha, *One Unmasked Moment Causes Massive Surge Without Protection and Tests*, Washington Post, August 29, 2021, Elementary school outbreak shows delta's risks for ...Washington Post https://www.washingtonpost.com › health › 2021/08/28.

100 ROGERS, *supra* note 11, at 67. This book discusses externalities in Part III, the Analysis portion of this book.

101 *Id.* at 216, citing to Robert P. Murphy, THE POLITICALLY INCORRECT GUIDE TO CAPITALISM at 7.

Therefore, in Part III of this book, we shall provide an analysis that considers the pros and cons of regulation in the 19 areas we mentioned in the Introduction and Overview.

The Trump Administration's approach to government regulation—consistent with the general Republican party narrative—is that "regulation and economic activity are inversely related." In other words, "less regulation always means more economic growth." On the other hand, those who generally identify as Democrats view "smart" regulation of the economy as producing a net increase in economic productivity.[102]

## G. Government Regulation That Seeks to Respond to Externalities as Impinging on Freedom

Most government regulation concerns efforts to respond to externalities[103] and the reduction of transaction costs for consumers.[104]

Government regulations that seek to reduce transaction costs include the regulation of businesses and professions. The goal of such regulations is to set industry-wide standards and to make information generally available to consumers.[105]

Other significant areas of government regulation include regulation of pollution and other environmental concerns[106]; regulation of natural monopolies (e.g., producers of electricity)[107], regulation believed to be necessary to allocate inherently scarce resources (e.g., broadcast frequency regulation, regulation of the geosynchronous satellite zone, regulation of common grazing areas, etc.),[108] social justice regulations (e.g., antidiscrimination laws),[109] and social welfare

---

102  Catherine Rampell, *supra* note 46, at A19.
103  HARRISON, *supra* note 1, at 335; ROGERS, *supra* note 11, at 6, 64–68.
104  HARRISON, *supra* note 1, at 328–335. *See also* at 77–103.
105  *Id.* at 328–335.
106  *Id.* at 40.
107  *Id.* at 306–325.
108  *Id.* at 325–327.
109  *Id.* at 342–345.

legislation that the government implements through its power to coercively take people's money through the implementation of taxes.[110]

## H. Spending Taxpayer Money on Welfare, Safety, and Other Programs

Conservative economist Robert P. Murphy argues that when government intervenes in the capitalist free market system of supply and demand, "it not only tramples on freedom, and individual rights, but also often hurts the very people it presumes to help."[111]

Every government tax and spending program has some redistributive effect. Many government welfare programs, for instance, seem designed to help a relatively small group of people such as the poor. But other programs benefit the relatively rich.[112] Accordingly, in every government tax and spending program, there will be net beneficiaries of the program or net contributors.[113]

The concept of "economic efficiency" has two major competing factions—one which emphasizes distortions created by the government (and remedied by decreasing the role of government) and distortions caused by markets (and reduced by increasing government involvement).[114]

Most commonly, economic efficiency (*which considers ideas of equality and distributive justice as irrelevant in reaching its conclusions*) is contrasted with government welfare economics (*which involves trade-offs between efficiency and distributive justice*).[115]

It is inevitable that people will ultimately end up as either net contributors or net recipients in essentially every government distribution program. Thus, issues of fairness—i.e., the government's use of its taxing powers to take a larger amount of money from one group of persons to give to another group

---

110 ROGERS, *supra* note 11, at 23, 41–45, 47–53, 101–102.

111 *Id.* 113 at 216.

112 HARRISON, *supra* note 1, at 444–445.

113 *Id.* at 437.

114 ROGERS, *supra* note 11, at 95.

115 *Id.*

of persons—underly much of the debate. Therefore, the goal of government welfare economics is to address issues of economic inequality and economic efficiency in such a manner that those who become better off as a result of a government policy or program only receive a benefit to the extent that those at the bottom of the distribution chain (in some instances, the more affluent) also are made better off.[116]

The thesis of this book is that a system of regulated capitalism operating under a government welfare economic approach to capitalism is the best way to ensure a better future for all people. It is the system followed by all developed capitalistic nations in the West. Historically, however, countries associated with the European Union have been stronger adherents to the philosophy underlying government welfare economics than the United States.

## I. Is Government Really Necessary?

A threshold question that must be addressed is why people choose to have a government in the first place. In this context, government means "an environment in which one will not have free rein to exercise all of one's choices."[117]

Thus, the term government "implies that there is some element of control by the government."[118]Accordingly, people consent to an actual or potential loss of liberty in establishing a government. This is because forming a government is "a necessary part of an implicit contract with others who will be similarly limited." In other words, the opportunity cost[119] in forming a government is what "people must give up to induce the cooperation of others."[120]

"This discussion suggests that people may consent to being governed essentially because they are better off under a body of laws." In other words, "there are some circumstances under which a system of government is more

---

116 ROGERS, *supra* note 11, at 7–10.
117 HARRISON, *supra* note 1, at 429.
118 *Id.*
119 ROGERS, *supra* note 11, at 4–5, 62, 223–234.
120 HARRISON, *supra* note 1, at 435.

efficient than a 'state of nature' or the absence of government. The amount of personal liberty individuals are willing to cede will be, in theory, determined by weighing the value of that liberty against the value to be gained pooling each person's liberty in a 'government.'"[121]

The most common risk in a context in which there is majority control, however, is that one will find that he or she is part of a minority whose freedoms must be limited to satisfy or increase the utility of the majority. Supreme Court cases such as *Bowers v. Hardwick*,[122] *Korematsu v. United States*,[123] and *Plessy v. Ferguson*,[124] all illustrate that in a utilitarian world, there will be losers as well as winners.[125]

## J. The Ironies of Freedom, Liberty, Sovereignty, and Neoliberalism

In her book, *Ugly Freedoms*, Professor Elisabeth Anker, discusses how people and entities often rely on notions of freedom, liberty, personal sovereignty, government sovereignty, and neoliberalism as grounds to be free of government regulation. Ironically, people and entities have also used these same concepts to suppress or even destroy the liberty of others throughout the history of the United States of America.

In the introduction to her book, Anker notes some of the ironies of freedom and liberty.

She states that "[f]reedom is a notoriously contested concept" as its meaning has been used to justify and legitimize the domination of one group of people over others. This domination includes "slavery, indigenous dispossession, environmental destruction, sex and gender oppression, and the violent machinations of a 'free' market that enable the powerful few to accumulate

---

121  HARRISON, *supra* note 1, at 432.
122  478 U.S. 186 (1986).
123  323 U.S. 214 (1944).
124  163 U.S. 537 (1896).
125  HARRISON, *supra* note 1, at 437.

vast wealth amid widespread poverty and homelessness."[126] Accordingly, freedom often "ignores the appalling violence that traffics under its name."[127]

Anker notes that some scholars even view the emancipation of former slaves as a continuing tragedy because of the **unfreedoms that remain** after and through the emancipation process.[128] They contend that emancipation was actually a reformulation of racialized unfreedom, undergirded by White supremacy.[129]

In their view, the notion of emancipation represents only a *mythic march of freedom* in which the story of emancipation "(1) places Black unfreedom in the past, (2) claims uninterrupted progress to the present, or (3) names Lincoln and/or other White actors, including the White body politic, its main protagonists."[130]

Indeed, the foundational philosophies of freedom set forth by Locke, Mill and Kant, "combine visions of emancipation for unjust authority with justification of despotism and inequality for 'uncivilized' nonwhite peoples; indeed, they make racial exclusion the condition for their universal visions."[131]

On the other hand, Anker notes that political liberals and progressives seem to view "freedom as a collective work to compose a shared world across differences between people without exploitation or domination."[132] They also seem to view freedom as the right to be free from the arbitrary control of another.[133]

Anker states that anti-mask protesters based their position on the grounds of individual freedom against government paternalism. However, Anker notes that they do not accept responsibility for the world outside of their "constructed private sphere." Instead, they disdain a version of freedom grounded on "shared

---

126 ANKER, *supra* note 1, at 2 and 4.
127 *Id.* at 14.
128 ANKER, *supra* note 1, at 32.
129 *Id.* at 78.
130 *Id.* at 81.
131 *Id.* at 89–90.
132 *Id.*
133 *Id.* at 19.

independence, collective accountability, and a bodily dignity that stands in solidarity with the most vulnerable as an expression of mutuality."[134]

## 1. Liberty

Anker recounts the story of an American soldier who penned a song that soldiers sang while waterboarding Filipino captives during the U.S. war to annex the Philippines. The lyrics the soldiers sang stated that the soldiers were giving the victims of their torture a "taste of liberty" while shouting the "Battle Cry of Freedom." The writer of the song titled the song "The Water Cure in the P.I."[135] It is an example of the use of freedom to justify the domination of native people who had become the subjects of U.S. colonialism and imperialism. And it illustrates how practices of freedom have often included the unfettered right to cause harm to others on the basis of liberty, individual autonomy, and sovereignty.

## 2. Personal Sovereignty

Anker notes that sovereign power generally refers to "the final authority to make decisions about life and death within a given sphere." For example, Anker notes that "[g]un ownership carries the promise of strengthening personal freedom as individual sovereignty." Accordingly, "individual freedom practiced through gun ownership constructs political relationships through analytics of control and threat assessment rather than equality or cooperation." One commentator noted that this analysis, in conjunction with statutes such as Concealed Carry and Stand Your Ground invests people with the sovereign right to kill.[136]

Scholars and commentators have viewed the right to own personal property, territorial control over people and their practices, and human exceptionalism as expressions of sovereignty.[137]

---

134 *Id.* at 8–9.
135 *Id.* at 1–2:
136 *Id.* at 10.
137 *Id.* at 18.

Anker notes that John Stuart Mill stated that the only limit to individual freedom was that a person's freedom could not be exercised to do harm to another. However, freedom-based rationales for anti-masking and gun carrying rights are now expressed by their very capacity to harm others.[138]

The Supreme Court's decision in the case of *Dobbs v. Jackson Women's Health Organization*,[139] in which the Court gave the politicians in each state the right to determine whether a woman should have the right to terminate a pregnancy, is a classic example of state sovereignty, in the abortion context. This is because the Supreme Court authorized state politicians to have the "the final authority to make decisions" about whether a woman should have the right to terminate a pregnancy.[140]

### *3. Liberty & Sovereignty as the Right of Persons to Destroy the Planet for Individual, Short-Term Gain*

The American ideal of freedom—which involves control over nature, individual sovereignty, human exceptionalism, uncoerced will, and private ownership—"is partly accountable for the geological upheaval and toxic pollution of climate change." As Anker puts it, under this version of freedom, "control of nature becomes an indication of personal sovereignty, and collective action to care for the earth seems a coercive limit on individual agency."[141] In Anker's view, neoliberalism and climate change are in a partnership that is rapidly destroying habitats and burning the world "under freedom's mantle."[142]

Indeed, human activities, Anker notes, "have already killed and displaced hundreds of millions of people and are poised to kill billions more living creatures from bees to plankton." And some calculate that human activity is responsible for the death of over a dozen animals and plant species every day.[143]

---

138 *Id.* at *Id.* 11.
139 597 U.S. __, 142 S.Ct. 2228 (2022).
140 ANKER, *supra* note 1, at 10.
141 *Id.* at 33.
142 *Id.* at 35.
143 *Id.* at 49.

To the wealthy residents of Rancho Santa Fe, California, water use is a form of freedom that justified their refusal to comply with voluntary water restrictions imposed by the government during the drought in southern California from 2015–2017.[144] These wealthy residents argued that they had purchased the freedom to use water in any quantity they wished and that this personal choice was an integral element of their individual liberty. Not surprisingly, when the State reacted to the community's refusal to voluntarily comply and imposed mandatory restrictions, the inhabitants of Rancho Santa Fe began to use even more water. Indeed, some called the mandatory restrictions an act of war; and others said that "we're not all equal when it comes to water."[145]

Anker states that the arguments made by the inhabitants of Rancho Santa Fe, are based on the notion of **"freedom as consumptive sovereignty."**[146] Anker points out that "consumptive sovereignty ties high consumption to the exercise of freedom, to sovereign control over oneself and ones property, and to domination over objects, people, and resources as an expression of agentic subjectivity."[147] Anker also notes that the concept of consumptive sovereignty **empowers people with the sense that they have the right to opt out of collective problems.**[148]

In this sense, Anker notes that we are all Ranchero. This can happen when we "drive to work when we could take public transportation or bike, when we order products from Amazon, when we forget to turn off the air conditioning, or even when we buy a new item of clothing. . . ." Accordingly, when we engage in this type of behavior, Anker states that "we damage the environment with thoughtless patterns of consumption; [and] we prioritize individual choice and personal ease over public needs and the flourishing of shared ecosystems."[149]

---

144 *Id.* at 153–154, 155, 156.
145 *Id.* at 154.
146 *Id.* at 153–155.
147 *Id.* at 156–157.
148 *Id.* at 157.
149 *Id.* at 159.

Anker also notes that: "[i]n this version of freedom, territorial borders demarcate the practice of freedom" and "fix freedom's limit." Conceptually, the adherents to this view consider these borders to be "sovereign boundaries, both of the self and of property—private and self-determining spaces" over which a person has exclusive authority.[150]

Thus, for example, those who champion the concept of consumptive sovereignty—regardless of whether their actions may harm others and, indeed, the entire world—believe that regulatory restrictions on their behavior constitute an infringement on their individual freedom. Consequently, they subscribe to "the neoliberal insistence" that government regulation represents coercion of free choice.[151]

The late physicist, Stephen Hawking, also theorized that humans would turn the planet into a giant ball of fire by 2600 due to overcrowding and energy consumption, which will make Earth uninhabitable.

As a result, Hawking believed that humans will need to go to live on another planet. Hawking said humans will need to colonize another planet within 100 years or face extinction.

In a BBC documentary in 2017, Hawking stated that "[w]ith climate change, overdue asteroid strikes, epidemics and population growth, our own planet is [in] an increasingly precarious" state of danger.[152]

## 4. Liberalism and Neoliberalism

Anker states that liberalism is the most widely influential theory of freedom in Western political thought.[153] Indeed, the dominant political and economic thought in the U.S. until the 1930s—the classical school of economics (sometimes referred to as classical liberalism)—defined liberty to mean individual

---

150 *Id.* at 155.

151 *Id.* at 156.

152 *Stephen Hawking predictions: Human extinction to global warming* www.cnbc.com/2018/03/15/stephen-hawking...

153 *Id.* at 20.

freedom from government interference and regulation, and the ability to organize relationships on the basis of free contracts between consenting adults. Classical liberals argued that individual freedom is more important than the welfare of society as a group.[154]

However, in the 1930s, Keynesian Economics[155] ended the dominance of classical economics in America. Nevertheless, Friedrich Hayek and Milton Friedman led a revival of interest in classical liberalism in the 20th century. Commentators refer to this movement as "neoclassical liberalism."[156]

In the first chapter of her book, Anker focuses on freedom's violent practices as witnessed through the Barbados sugar plantations' entrepreneurial and ruthless exercise of bodily control over their slaves in the 1600s. Anker notes that the history of the Barbadian sugar plantations is necessary to understand the contours of how liberalism developed in America to support chattel slavery.[157]

Specifically, Anker notes that John Locke—liberalism's earliest foundational theorist—[158] justified the freedom of the Barbadian plantations to beat and kill slaves on the basis of profitmaking and political theories of individual freedom.[159] Indeed, John Locke and Peter Colleton used the Barbados system as the model in drafting the Fundamental Constitutions for the Carolinas in 1669.[160] That Constitution, among other things: (1) legalized chattel slavery; (2) "allowed every free man to have absolute dominion and power over his negro slaves;" and (3) granted "every free man" **sovereign authority,** including the power of life and death, over "his negro slaves."

The Fundamental Constitutions also justified the dispossession of uncultivated land occupied by indigenous people. Indeed, **Locke's labor theory of property** became a celebrated theoretical justification for disposing native

---

154 ROGERS, *supra* note 11, at 17–18, 199–200 (2016).

155 *Id.* at 203, 314–315.

156 *Id.* at 199.

157 ANKER, *supra* note 1, at 31, 37–64.

158 *Id.* at 41.

159 *Id.* at 31.

160 *Id.* at 61–63.

people of their real estate.[161] Most, if not all, law school real property case-books discuss Locke's labor theory of property as part of the class discussion.[162] As Anker notes: "Political theorists and historians have grappled with both Locke's personal involvement in colonialism and slavery and the implications of this involvement for the theories of liberal government.[163]

Anker notes that liberalism views negative freedom as the absence of constraint and coercion. Under this view, government should not interfere with a person's ability to make autonomous decisions. Positive freedom, on the other hand, is the ability of a person to act purposively guided by a vision for what freedom is and how to practice it, rather than merely the absence of interference. However, liberalism's focus on negative freedom enables a type of negative and positive freedom that enables persons to engage in exploitation and domination of others in ways that liberalism does not classify as coercion.[164]

Accordingly, sometimes, they base their positions on the right to be free *from* government regulation. However, on other occasions, they justify policies that may even cause them harm on the freedom *to* engage in certain activities.

Additionally, liberalism's focus on individualism and capitalism also posit that collective political action is primarily coercive in nature. It is for these reasons that progressives view neoliberalism and authoritarian politicians—who adhere to those views—as the cause of a significant erosion in support for social programs for the most vulnerable in society, as well as initiatives to tackle climate change. Accordingly, progressives now view their late 20th century hope of achieving "the promises of the American Dream and progress toward a cooperative world order as having slipped out of reach in the 21st century."[165]

John Stuart Mill's treatise, titled *On Liberty*, propelled modern liberal thought by "arguing for universal individual sovereignty limited only" by a

---

161 *Id.* at 57.

162 *See, e.g.,* DUKEMINIER, KRIER, ALEXANDER, SCHILL, PROPERTY 14–16 (2008).

163 ANKER, *supra* note 1, at 56.

164 *Id.* at 20–21.

165 *Id.* at 20–21, 27.

prohibition that a person could not exercise freedom in a manner that would cause harm to others. Yet, Mill championed the use of despotic imperialism against people deemed to be uncivilized and barbarians. Accordingly, Mill argued that practices involving the domination and subjugation of others could be compatible with freedom under certain circumstances.[166]

However, other commentators and scholars argue that freedom and violence are antagonistic. In other words, freedom ends where violence begins. Nevertheless, these same persons seem to agree that freedom can take shape as violence when fighting against domination.[167]

Anker agrees with the view of scholars, such as Wendy Brown, who state that "neoliberal polices entail 'wielding liberty claims' like weapons to dismantle social worlds and democratic practices that stand in the way of capital flows."[168]

Interestingly, neoliberalism depicts government as the primary source of unfreedom for persons. However, as Anker notes, neoliberalism "also intensifies state [i.e., government] power over the most insecure and marginalized segments of society." For example, Anker points out that government "[s]urveillance and [government] violence [directed toward working class people and the poor] have become essential aspects of the neoliberal management of escalating social and economic insecurity produced by decimated social safety nets and deregulated profitmaking."[169] Anker elaborates on this point, by noting:

This is partly why 'the land of the free' has the highest rates of incarceration in the world. Neoliberalism guards both the flow of wealth and the bodies of the wealthy from confrontation with the people it exploits and excludes. If, as Anthony Bogues argues, 'Freedom is the organizing language for neoliberalism,' it is a very specific type

---

166 *Id.* at 21.
167 *Id.* at 22–23, 24.
168 *Id.* at 113–114.
169 *Id.* at 114.

of freedom: in neoliberal systems, money, rather than people, must be set free.[170]

In Anker's view, neoliberalism "has been a central component of the changes in the political economy of capitalism . . . that has cause[d] skyrocketing levels of economic equality . . ." Anker states that neoliberalism has accomplished this through "**the deregulation of profitmaking, the privatization of public goods**, and **the reduction of state support for social services . . .**"[171] These three things, Anker says, work in combination to "foment freedom as the unconstrained movement of capital and free association of financial streams." This has led to "a despairing sense that neoliberalism threatens the very survival of the poor and stymies the construction of common, cooperative, and egalitarian social worlds, while granting capital free roam."[172]

Indeed, studies conducted by economists Gabriel Zucman and Emanuel Saez found that the neoliberal policies of Ronald Reagan witnessed the wealth of the top 0.1 percent in the United States going from 7 percent of the nation's wealth to 22 percent by 2014. This was more than the bottom 85 percent combined.[173]

The political and economic visions of liberalism—upward mobility, individual sovereignty, prosperity for the hardworking—seem to be no longer sustainable in a neoliberal order flush with economic inequality.[174] However, the appeal of liberalism—with its emphasis on society as a group of individual actors as opposed to society as a single group—continues to dominate over the alternative approach. The alternative approach focuses on collective and public action.[175] However, as Anker notes, contemporary critics of liberalism have failed to offer a concrete vision "for how the world could be better

---

170 *Id.* at 113.

171 *Id.* at 114.

172 *Id.*

173 W. SHERMAN ROGERS, THE AFRICAN AMERICAN ENTREPRENEUR: CHALLENGES AND OPPORTUNITIES IN THE TRUMP ERA 7–8 (2019).

174 ANKER, *supra* note 1 at 117, 144.

175 *Id.* at 144.

organized."[176] In other words, there does not seem to be anything better at this point to the system of regulated capitalism operating under a government welfare economic approach utilized by all developed capitalistic nations in the West.[177]

In view of the lack of any specific, workable alternatives to liberalism—other than those which currently exist—Anker makes the following inquiry: "How do people act without inspiring promises of a free society on the horizon, without investing in the debunked narratives of progress and upward mobility, but also without succumbing to nihilism, capitulation, or defeat?[178] One thing that the United States can minimally do is to improve its social safety net to provide for universal healthcare, housing, daycare, and greater subsidies for food.[179]

---

176 *Id.* at 117, 144.
177 ROGERS, *supra* note 11, at 95–96.
178 ANKER, *supra* note 1, at 117.
179 ROGERS, *supra* note 11, at 121–127.

VEXATIOUS NEIGHBORS

# PART III

# ANALYSIS

## A. Government Regulation as a Response to Externalities: The Regulation of Actions by One Person That Negatively Affect Others When the Person Producing the Negative Affect Does not Compensate Those Harmed or When Persons Receiving a Positive Affect From the Actions of a Person Do Not Compensate the Person Who Produces the Positive Affect

### 1. When Does an Externality Exist?

*An externality exists when* (1) a person's (or a firm's) actions either negatively affect or positively affect another person or firm and (2) (a) the person causing the negative affect does not compensate the person negatively affected or (b) the person who benefits from a third person's actions does not compensate the person causing the positive affect.[180]

Accordingly, externalities narrowly refer to those negative or positive affects that are neither compensated (in the case of one who creates a negative affect who does not compensate the party harmed) nor rewarded (in the case of a person who receives a positive affect from a person but who does not reward

---

180 JEFFREY HARRISON and JULES THEEUWES, LAW AND ECONOMICS 58–63 (2008).

51

the person who has created the positive affect).[181] As a result, externalities can cause inefficiencies and market failures.[182]

## 2. George F. Wills, Jab at Progressives' Desire to Regulate Externalities

Columnist George F. Will wrote an article in the *Washington Post* that opined that excessive government regulation of human behavior was stifling, enervating, and devitalizing human society. He stated, in a tongue-in-cheek passage, that if progressive politicians determine that "taking a shower" or "eating a cheeseburger" or any other activity "affects others," these progressives are likely to mandate that government should regulate that behavior.[183]

In Will's view, "[t]here must be limits to prophylactic measures against even clear and present dangers." Otherwise, "public health officials," "excitable environmentalists," and those in charge of providing "safety" standards "from life's dangers" "will meet no resistance to the primal urge of all government agencies: the urge to maximize their missions."

Will states that government officials use public health, safety, and welfare threats as "an excuse for the minute supervision of life's quotidian activities." Will believes that there is a danger to liberty from what he refers to as "the excessive pursuit of safety from life's dangers." Perhaps Will states the best summary of his view on government regulation by his statement that the state should not attempt to shield people from all of "life's elemental realities and trade-offs."[184]

Will cites various authorities for the proposition that the U.S. has a tendency to create inflexible procedural rules that lead to "rule stupor." He states that this leads to:

---

181  Id. at 59.

182  ROGERS, *supra* note 11, at 64–65. *See also* at 59–61.

183  George F. Will, *Witness How Progressives Forfeit the Public's Trust*, WASH. POST, February 10, 2022, at A21, Witness how progressives in government forfeit the public's …*Washington Post* https://www.washingtonpost.com › 2022/02/09 › how....

184  *Id.*

the mechanical implementation of an ever-thickening web of regulations that leaves no room for untidy discretion.[185]

Perhaps, this is the reason why Will notes that in 1930, it took builders only 1 year and 45days to erect the Empire State Building while it took contractors in Georgia 14 years to complete an infrastructure project due to environmental and regulatory hurdles.[186]

As we proceed through this analysis, we shall address the pros and cons of regulation in specific instances. Underlying the discussion are the frequent clashes between the desire of persons to be free of regulation and the need to protect the health, safety and welfare of society.

### 3. Types of Externalities

In their book, *Law and Economics*,[187] Jeffrey L. Harrison and Jules Theeuwes, list ten different types of externalities (1) Beneficial (positive) (2) Harmful (negative); (3) Unidirectional (upstream activity negatively affecting persons downstream); (4) Reciprocal (traffic congestion); (5) Two person (neighbors); (6)Many persons (traffic and air pollution); (7) Affecting utility (noisy neighbor); (8) Affecting Production (overfishing); (9) Public (greenhouse effect) and (10) Private (smoking in a restaurant).[188]

### 4. How Externalities Create Inefficiencies

A manufacturer, for example, will impose social costs on society (e.g., pollution) if no one requires that the manufacturer pay for these costs (i.e., when there

---

185 *Id.*

186 George F. Will, *Can America Do Big Things Again? supra* note 47; About NYC's Most Famous Building | Empire State Building, https://www.esbnyc.com/about#:~:text=Construction%20was%20completed%20in%20a,1%20year%20and%20 45%20days.&text=Beautiful%20inside%20and%20out%2C%20the,marvel%20 beloved%20across%20the%20world.

187 HARRISON and THEEUWES, *supra* note 1, at 67.

188 *Id.* at 62.

is no requirement that the manufacturer incur **private costs**). *Consequently, the manufacturer will produce more of the good than it otherwise would if it had to pay for all of the costs of its production.* Therefore, the **marginal social cost** that the manufacturer imposes on society through its polluting activities (by producing the last unit of the good) will exceed its **marginal social benefit**. This is because **external costs**—for example, the manufacturer's pollution in the illustration—*by definition are never paid by the person who is imposing them on others.*[189]

Accordingly, market failures[190] and inefficiencies may occur in such situations. In the case of the polluting factory, **the level of pollution is allocative inefficient because the manufacturer will produce more pollution than it otherwise would if it had to pay for all of the costs of its production.**[191]

Consumers can also impose external costs on others in society. A classic example involves people who drive cars. A person who drives a car incurs *private costs* (fuel, maintenance, insurance, etc.) but also imposes *external costs* on others by adding to highway congestion, air pollution, wildlife degradation, and other societal costs. Because the driver does not pay for these external costs, he tends to consume more of the privilege of driving than he would if he had to pay for the social costs that he imposes on others.[192]

Accordingly, here is the key concept to remember. **If external costs are greater than 0, then private costs (i.e., the actual expenses incurred) that one must pay to engage in an activity will be less than the social costs imposed on others.** When this occurs, society tends to (1) price the good or service too low and (2) produce or consume too much of the good or service.

---

189 ROGERS, *supra* note 11, at 64–65.

190 *Id.* at 30–31, 59–60. Market failure takes when a voluntary exchange is "exceedingly costly or practically impossible" to consummate. *Id.* at 59. Accordingly, most economists concede a role for government in such cases. This is because private firms would not find it economically feasible to provide the services necessary to deliver a public good (e.g., a country's national defense, mandatory public education for all children, and a country's national highway system). This is because there would be too many free riders who would not pay a private firm to deliver such services. *Id.* at 59–60.

191 *Id.* at 64–65.

192 *Id.*

Accordingly, market failures may occur at the local, state, national, or even international levels.[193]

The way to address this problem is to require that the person causing the externality pay for it. Society can accomplish this result by requiring that the person or entity that produces the externality add **the marginal externality cost (MEC)** to the producer's marginal cost. The sum of the marginal cost and the marginal externality cost is called **the social marginal cost curve.**[194] This will cause society to produce or consume less of the good or service that causes the negative externality.

Economic efficiency is important because people generally want to maximize their net benefits. Net benefits equals total benefits minus total costs. When an economy is efficient, it is getting the best value for the least cost. A competitive economy is said to be **allocative efficient** and produces the greatest net benefit to society when the producers of goods and services in a country *increase the quantity* of a good or service they produce until the *price level* they charge equals *the marginal cost* (i.e., the supply price) they incurred to produce the good and the marginal cost equals *the marginal benefit* to consumers (i.e., the demand price that consumers are willing to pay for the good).[195]

At the point where marginal benefit equals marginal cost, the *demand price* of consumers (i.e., the marginal benefit) will equal the *supply price* incurred by producers (i.e., the marginal cost) resulting in a net benefit to both consumers and producers (referred to as **total surplus**) that will be at the highest possible level. Indeed, everyone benefits at this magical point as there will be a surplus going to consumers (**consumer surplus**) and a surplus going to producers (**producer surplus**).[196]

One of the bedrock justifications for government regulation is the existence of a natural monopoly. This is because a monopolist will be tempted to

---

193 *Id.*
194 HARRISON and THEEUWES, *supra* note 1, at 68–72.
195 ROGERS, *supra* note 11, at 16–17, 193–195.
196 *Id.*

produce a quantity of the good or service that stops when marginal revenue equals marginal cost and not when marginal benefit (i.e., the demand price) equals marginal cost (i.e., the supply price). When producers stop producing extra quantity when marginal revenue equals marginal cost instead of continuing to produce until marginal benefit equals marginal cost, the total surplus going to society will decrease. Therefore, the goal of achieving economic efficiency (Pareto optimal)—i.e., production until the marginal benefit equals the marginal cost—is one of the driving forces in the government's regulation of monopolies.[197]

## 5. Remedies for Externalities

### a. Externalities and Property Rights

The law's reaction to externalities helps to define what is meant by private property.[198]

The United States Constitution prohibits both state and federal governments from denying any person of life, liberty, and property without due process of law. But what exactly is the definition of "property"—this vitally important interest protected by the Due Process Clause of the United States Constitution? The answer is simple. Property is anything of value that the law permits one to acquire.[199]

It is law that determines what is property and who can own it.[200] Moreover, the concept of property is more expansive than some may realize. Property refers to more than mere objects and things. The Supreme Court has stated

---

197 *Id.* at 194–195. *See also* HARRISON, *supra* note 1, at 306–308.

198 HARRISON and THEEUWES, *supra* note 1, at 58.

199 *See* JEREMY BENTHAM, THEORY OF LEGISLATION, 111–13 (4th ed. 1882) ("Property and laws are born together, and die together. Before laws were made there was no property; take away laws and property ceases.").

200 For example, the Thirteenth Amendment to the United States Constitution removed the ability of one person to lawfully own another person as property. U.S. CONST. amend. XIII.

that property also confers a bundle of rights on its lawful owners.[201] Those rights include the right to *possess, use, exclude, and dispose* of one's property.[202]

This raises the question of how persons—both individual persons as well as entities recognized as juridical persons—protect their property rights? The law recognizes three ways in which persons can protect their property rights. This takes place through (1) property rules; (2) liability rules; and (3) rules of inalienability.[203] The court will typically issue an injunction to prohibit the interference with a person's property rights.[204]

*Property rules* mandate that no person may interfere with the property owner's property rights unless the property owner initially gives permission to the other person.[205]

*Liability rules* do not mandate that a person first obtain a property owner's rights before interfering with the property owner's rights. However, the law requires that the person who interferes with the property owner's rights pay damages to the property owner.[206]

*Inalienability rules* provide that a property owner may not transfer nor may another person acquire the property owner's property regardless of the property owner's consent.[207] Examples of entitlements that cannot be generally sold include: (1) a person's internal body organs; (2) a person's right to vote; and (3) a person's ability to have sex with others.[208]

The reason why the government prohibits persons from selling these three entitlements for compensation is typically because society considers

---

201 *See, e.g.,* Kaiser Aetna v. United States, 444 U.S. 164, 176 (1979); Superior Bath House Co. v. McCarroll, 312 U.S. 176, 180–81 (1941).

202 *See generally* Moore v. Regents of Univ. of California, 793 P.2d 479, 509 (Cal. 1990) (Mosk, J., dissenting) (explaining that the bundle of property rights surrounding one's bodily tissue could be broken up into component rights rather than using the all or nothing analysis of the majority).

203 HARRISON and THEEUWES, *supra* note 1, at 55–56, 94–96, 383.

204 HARRISON, *supra* note 1, at 98–99, 368.

205 *Id.* at 55–56. 94–96, 383.

206 *Id.*

207 *Id.*

208 HARRISON, *supra* note 1, at 102–103.

selling them to be morally repugnant, and to have a negative effect on society. Additionally, the government sometimes bases its prohibition on paternalistic justifications grounded on the belief that the parties to the exchange do not know what is best for them.[209]

## b. Remedies For Externalities.

### (1) Remedies for Negative Externalities

Remedies to address negative externalities involve "specific ways to reduce the inefficient, high level of production and concomitant high level of a negative externality (e.g., pollution)."[210]

There are two remedies used to adjust production and pollution to efficient levels. They are (1) pricing remedies and (2) command and control remedies.[211]

The basic idea underlying *the pricing remedy* is that the polluter must pay for the pollution that the polluter causes and, thus, internalize these costs. The key thing to remember is that when the polluter must pay a price for the polluter's damage to the environment, it *increases the polluter's production costs and, as a result, will cause the polluter to produce less* of the harmful product.

*Command and control remedies* have an advantage over pricing remedies in that they are precise and certain in their effects. However, command and control remedies can also be inefficient. For example, "[i]f the government commands firms to install a certain piece of equipment to clean up exhaust pipes," this mandate "might not always be the most cost-efficient piece of equipment available." However, if "the government works with a tradable permit, it provides firms with an incentive to install the most cost-efficient equipment."[212]

---

209 *Id.*
210 HARRISON and THEEUWES, *supra* note 1, at 73–80.
211 *Id.* at 73.
212 *Id.* at 77.

**There are three basic forms of pricing remedies for negative externalities:**

- **Environmental Taxes.** For example, "[i]f the government decides that all producers of kitchen sink cleaners have to pay an environmental tax of $0.50 per bottle, then this environmental tax is a perfect remedy."[213]

- **Tradable emission permits.** This remedy assumes, for example, that a government's environmental agency has determined that producers can safely discharge a certain amount of a pollutant into a river (e.g., ten thousand tons) per year without endangering public safety. Thereafter, the government could issue ten thousand permits for one ton of pollutant in the river per year. One permit could, for example, allow a polluting firm to discharge one ton of pollutant into the river per year and discharging without a permit would carry a stiff fine.[214]

The government would, subsequently, offer these permits for sale and allow the firms to trade the permits. Supply and demand would determine the price for the permits. Firms that can reduce their discharge level at a low cost (e.g., by installing equipment) could offer their permits for sale. These firms would be able to make money from selling permits if they can sell permits at a price that is higher than the cost of reducing their level of discharge.[215]

- **Abatement subsidies.** This remedy requires that the government subsidize firms for installing abatement or cleaning equipment to reduce pollution. When the government subsidizes the cost of the abatement equipment, it solves the externality problem without creating a necessity for a price increase by the firm on the international market. Otherwise, the home firm would have to raise its prices and

---

213 *Id.* at 70–71, 73–74. We also discussed this earlier in the text corresponding to note 194.
214 *Id.* at 76.
215 *Id.*

might lose substantial export revenues to international firms whose countries are not concerned about pollution externalities in those countries.[216]

**Similarly, there are three basic forms of command-and-control remedies to address negative externalities:**

- Government requirements for the installation of **abatement technology.** The government, for example, might make it mandatory for firms in a particular industry to "[i]nstall flue glass desulphurization equipment."[217]

- Government limitations on **emission rates.** In this instance, the government might require, for example, that firms limit the amount of effluents to "no more than 10 mg of pollutant X per 1000 gallons discharged."[218]

- Government limitations on **emission levels.** In this situation, the government may order plant Y to limit its emissions to no more than Z tons of pollutant X in any month.[219]

### (2) Remedies for Positive Externalities

On the other hand, remedies to address positive externalities involve specific ways to compensate persons whose actions provide a benefit to others. For example, the government may pass laws to ensure that an inventor of a revolutionary technology receives compensation for the inventor's innovative product. This is why the government enacted patent, trademark, and copyright

---

216 *Id.* at 77.
217 *Id.* at 73.
218 *Id.*
219 *Id.*

laws. Otherwise, free riders would take advantage of the producer's products without having to pay the producer for those benefits.[220]

## B. The Arguments for and Against Regulation in 19 Situations

The book *Winners and Losers in the American Capitalistic Economy: A Primer*, among other things, critiques approximately 22 government laws that conservative economist, Robert P. Murphy maintains are not necessary under a system of pure capitalism. This book discusses several of Murphy's assertions.[221] The book also discusses several contemporary issues that involve arguments that rely on a person's right to be free of government rules and regulations.

At the bottom of these arguments is the question of whether government regulation of market activity "tramples on freedom and individual rights. . . ."[222] In the following 19 examples, we shall seek to ascertain each instance in which persons and entities seek to be exempt from regulation on the basis of arguments which rely on either concepts of freedom, liberty, neoliberalism, and State and/or individual sovereignty.

Underlying the discussion are the frequent clashes between the desire of persons to be free of government regulation versus the role of government to protect society generally and, occasionally, certain vulnerable segments of society. The desire to be free from government regulation is consistent with neoliberalism's definition of liberty as individual freedom from government regulation, and the ability to organize relationships on the basis of free contracts between consenting adults.[223]

*The goal in discussing these examples is not to provide an in-depth analysis of these topics.* That is beyond the scope of this book. Indeed, you may not be particularly interested in the underlying subject matter of some of the examples. Rather, *the sole objective in exploring these nineteen examples is to illustrate how*

---

220  *Id.* at 80. *See also* ROGERS, *supra* note 11, at 66.
221  *See generally*, ROGERS, *supra* note 11, at 215–245.
222  *Id.* at 216.
223  *Id.* at 17–18, 199–200.

*people and entities use notions of freedom, liberty, personal sovereignty, government sovereignty, and neoliberalism as grounds to be free of government regulation and/ or to suppress the liberty of others.*

Accordingly, this book will provide just enough information for the reader to, hopefully, be able to understand the subject matter involved in the examples for the ultimate purpose of illustrating the arguments advanced by some against government regulation of their actions in the context of these examples. With this in mind, let's begin our analysis.

## 1. Helmet Law Cases as an Example of Liberty-Based Arguments to be Free of Government Regulation

Cases involving helmet laws serve as a great illustration of the liberty-based arguments against helmet regulations. For years, people have fought against helmet laws as violating their freedom to ride their bikes without a helmet. "It's all about freedom. Freedom of choice, freedom of expression, right to privacy, and now, freedom of religion." And, yet, it is undisputable that helmets save lives and economic costs.[224] On the other hand, if a bike rider suffers a preventable brain injury, the public at large eventually pays for their healthcare.[225]

Prior to 1966, no state in the United States had enacted a motorcycle helmet law.[226] States initially enacted universal motorcycle helmet laws in 1966 because the federal government required this action as a prerequisite for states to receive federal highway construction funds. And by 1975, forty-seven states and the District of Columbia had passed such laws. The helmet laws were controversial from the beginning and motorcycle groups unsuccessfully fought the laws in the courts.

---

224  *See* Melissa Newman, *supra* note 44, at 215
225  *Id.*
226  *Id.* at 217.

However, ten years later, in 1976, Congress eliminated the federal funding incentive.[227] As of 2008, only twenty states required helmets for all motorcycle riders while the remaining states either did not have helmet laws or only had partial laws that typically required helmets for riders less than eighteen years of age.[228]

Those who oppose helmet laws do so on the basis of individual freedom against government paternalism, personal sovereignty to make final decisions about life and death, and the primacy of individual choice over public needs.[229]

### 2. Whether State Government Sovereignty Should be a Basis for Restricting a Woman's Nearly 50-year Liberty-Based Right to Terminate a Pregnancy

In *Dobbs v. Jackson Women's Health Organization*,[230] the U.S. Supreme Court held that the Fourteenth Amendment's reference to "liberty" does not protect the right of women to have an abortion. In the Court's view, abortion is different from other rights based on a person's right to privacy and ability to make personal choices that are central to a person's dignity and autonomy.

The Court noted that "none" of the Court's prior cases based on liberty rights "involved the critical moral question posed by abortion." Unlike the other liberty-based rights the Court protected in other cases, only abortion permitted the destruction of what *Roe* termed "potential life" and what the challenged Mississippi law referred to as the killing of an "unborn human being."[231] The Court stated that it was this critical moral question that made the issue of abortion "unique."[232] For this reason, the Court held that the legislatures of the states had the right to determine for women whether women

---

227  *Id.* at 215–216.

228  *Id.* at 215.

229  Mandatory Helmet Laws—Freedom Or Safety Issue?
EatSleepRIDE https://eatsleepride.com › mandatory_helmet_laws_-_f . . . , *supra* note 41.

230  597 U.S. __, 142 S.Ct. 2228 (2022).

231  *Id.* at 2257–2258.

232  *Id.* at 2277.

residing in a particular state should be allowed to terminate a pregnancy and under what circumstances, if any. Accordingly, the Court held that the sovereign rights of state legislatures outweighed the liberty of a woman to choose to terminate a pregnancy.[233]

Arguments based on freedom, personal sovereignty, state sovereignty (as illustrated in the *Dobbs* case), and neoliberalism, typically depict government as the primary source of unfreedom. However, as we noted at the outset of this book, these lofty concepts have been used to allow government to suppress or even destroy the liberty of persons deemed unworthy of protection. The *Dobbs* case is a powerful illustration of this point as the Court permitted state sovereigns, if they wished, to suppress the liberty rights of women to terminate a pregnancy.

### 3. Whether the Government Should be Able to Dictate That People Wear Masks and Take Vaccines During the Global Pandemic?

Opponents of vaccine and mask requirements have filed federal lawsuits that challenge Covid-19 shutdowns, mask mandates, vaccine mandates, the safety of vaccines, and even whether the virus is a real safety issue. Organizations such as Make America Free Again have funded much of the litigation.[234]

They view their position as a "medical freedom fight"; characterize government leaders enforcing coronavirus regulations as scumbags; and liken "vaccine mandates to the authoritarianism of apartheid era South Africa and Nazi Germany."[235] And groups such as Feds for Medical Freedom and D.C. Firefighters Bodily Autonomy Affirmation Group were among the

---

233 *Id.* at 2277, 2284.

234 Shawn Boburg, John Swaine, *Vaccine Skepticism Breeds a New Celebrity: Ohio Lawyer's Rise Shows How Misinformation Can Fuel Fundraising, Renown*, WASH. POST, September 21, 2021, at A1.
One lawyer's rise shows how vaccine misinformation can fuel ...Yahoo https://www .yahoo.com › amphtml › now › one-lawy

235 *Id.*

estimated 20,000 anti-vaccine activists attending a rally in Washington, D.C. on January 23, 2022.[236]

These arguments occasionally lead to contradictory positions on the nature of liberty and personal freedoms. For example, government leaders in Texas, who control all of the political branches of state government, vehemently oppose vaccine mandates. Their proffered reason for this position was based on the right of individuals to personal freedom and the liberty to choose what is in their best interests.

Yet, these same leaders passed legislation designed to deny that very liberty and freedom of choice to women in the context of abortion. In the view of one commentator, it appears that Texas Republicans, who control the executive and legislative branches of state government, have the unfettered right to determine who has freedom to choose and to impose "severe discriminatory burdens on a single class of people (pregnant women) solely because of their status."[237]

### 4. Should All Laws Prohibiting Discrimination be Abolished?

Economist Robert P. Murphy contends that the government did not need to pass anti-discrimination laws because the invisible hand of the market will punish discriminators.[238] Thus, for example, Murphy contends that an employer that discriminates on the basis of gender will lose $15,000 in potential profits if the female applicant would have produced $15,000 more in revenues than the male applicant.

---

236 *See* Peter Jamison, Ellie Silverman, *Anti-Vaccine Activists Hope Rally in D.C. Cements Gains: They've Used Pandemic to Spread Message That Many See as Dangerous,* WASH POST, January 23, 2022, at A1, Anti-vaccine activists see DC rally as a marker of recent gains *Washington Post*
https://www.washingtonpost.com › 2022/01/21 › anti-.
237 David Von Drehle, *The Texas Abortion Law is a Classic Case of Might-Makes-Right in Action*, September 5, 2021, at A23, Opinion | The Texas abortion law is a classic case of might- ...*Washington Post*
https://www.washingtonpost.com › 2021/09/03 › texas...
238 ROGERS, *supra* note 11, at 217.

This is in keeping with neoliberal teaching that frowns upon any government regulation that impinges on the ability of persons to use the resources they control to enter into bilateral, voluntary, and informed exchanges that are mutually acceptable to the parties to the bargain.[239]

This requires a system based on private property and the incentive for profit. The capitalist system, according to Murphy, will lead persons and entities to do what is best for themselves and society. Murphy contends that when government intervenes in the free market system of supply and demand, "it not only tramples on freedom, and individual rights, but also often hurts the very people it presumes to help."[240]

Murphy maintains that the government and unions are the real sources of race and gender discrimination. For example, Murphy states that the Davis-Bacon Act of 1931—which requires that federally funded construction contracts pay "locally prevailing wages"—prevented black workers from submitting low bids for federal construction contracts.[241]

### 5. Should the Government Regulate the Contamination of the Environment or Wildlife Conservation?

According to Murphy, the government did not need to pass laws regulating the contamination of the environment or to pass wildlife conservation laws. This is because, in his view, these laws are inefficient. Murphy argues that in a society with secure property rights in a reproducible resource, the property owner has an incentive to ensure the commodity's continued existence. Accordingly, free markets encourage conservation. In Murphy's view, this is how capitalism will save the environment. In contrast, when the government (or the public) owns a resource, it's just as if no one owns it. Therefore, there is little incentive to take action against those who threaten the commodity's existence. It is for these reasons that Murphy argues that government officials

---

239  *Id.* at 216.
240  *Id.*
241  *Id.* at 217–218.

in African countries have little incentive to prevent poachers of endangered species since they don't personally benefit from maintaining the stocks of these animals.[242]

Murphy notes that, today, just as farmers abused the unowned commons in earlier years, fishermen will continue to over fish the oceans and businesses will continue to overcut public timberlands in the absence of property rights in these unowned resources. Similarly, in a society with secure property rights, a company that dumped chemicals in a river would first need to make arrangements with the river's owners. Murphy also argues that the decision whether we should recycle a product or dump it is not a moral issue but an economic one. Accordingly, he states that if it would be cheaper to dispose of the used item and make a new one from virgin materials, it would be wasteful to recycle the product.[243]

Accordingly, Murphy maintains that market prices best determine the proper balance between whether we should recycle a product or dump it as opposed to arbitrary government campaigns. He also notes that "capitalist economies have enjoyed steady improvement in environmental quality, while the totalitarian governments have been the worst desecrators on the planet."[244]

However, Murphy does not directly address whether a decision based solely on secure property rights and business profits of private firms should outweigh other considerations such as the destruction of the planet as result of climate change. In the long run, the opportunity costs of leaving the protection of the environment to private business seems too high. As Elizabeth Anker stated, under this version of freedom, "control of nature becomes an indication of personal sovereignty, and collective action to care for the earth seems a coercive limit on individual agency."[245] In Anker's view, neoliberalism

---

242 *Id.* at 220–221.
243 *Id.*
244 *Id.* at 221–222.
245 ANKER, *supra* note 1, at 33.

and climate change are in a partnership that is rapidly destroying habitats and burning the world "under freedom's mantle."[246]

## 6. *Whether it was Wise for the Government to Enact Social Security Legislation?*

According to Murphy, the government did not need to enact Social Security legislation. Capitalism developed insurance products and savings and investment products for such purposes. Moreover, Social Security, in Murphy's view, is neither social nor is it secure. Instead, he characterizes Social Security as a giant Ponzi scheme in which current beneficiaries are being funded by subsequent contributors.[247]

Instead of Social Security, Murphy favors reliance on charitable organizations to address the issues of the needy, the unfortunate, and those whose recklessness or ignorance has reduced them to dependency on others.

Murphy, however, does not address the very real problem that private charity is not steady and is capable of drastic reductions or even stoppage. Murphy's view is consistent with the neoliberal view that freedom is more important than the welfare of society as a group.[248] It is for these reasons that progressives view neoliberalism as the cause of a significant erosion of support for social programs for the most vulnerable in society.[249]

## 7. *Whether it was Wise for the Government to Pass Any Anti-Poverty Laws?*

Murphy notes that one of the greatest objections to pure unbridled capitalism is that it produces income inequality. However, he contends that private philanthropy respects property rights, treats recipients with greater dignity,

---

246  *Id.* at 35.
247  ROGERS, *supra* note 11, at 222.
248  *Id.* at 199–200.
249  ANKER, *supra* note 1, at 21, 27.

and squanders fewer funds on overhead and fraud. Murphy points to statistics indicating that the poverty rate was steadily falling until Lyndon Johnson's Great Society programs in the 1960s. Since that time, the poverty rate has been roughly flat for the following thirty-five years.[250]

Murphy notes that most people concede that communism does not work well as an economic system. Instead, "they seek a middle ground that avoids the misery of communism as well as the allegedly unconscionable excesses of capitalism." In Murphy's view, it is debatable whether the $7 trillion spent on government anti-poverty programs between 1964 to 2007 has done anything to reduce poverty.

Interestingly, the research of epidemiologists Richard Wilson and Kate Pickett indicate that countries, like the U.S., that have greater economic inequality, spend less of their national income on social services than peer countries. The findings of Wilson and Pickett also found that the U.S. and other countries that spend less of their national income on social services had greater rates of teen pregnancy, infant mortality, mental illness, drug use, imprisonment, and homicide than countries where wealth is more evenly distributed.[251]

### 8. Whether it was Wise for the Government to Enact Any Antitrust Laws? And Whether the Antitrust Laws Should be Used to Thwart Certain Practices Utilized by Facebook, Amazon, Google, and Microsoft?

According to Murphy, a producer can only control a market under a system of pure capitalism if the firm provides a better product at a lower cost. He notes that dominant firms are always subject to competition from newcomers absent government privileges. In contrast, firms that turn to the

---

250 ROGERS, *supra* note 11, at 222.
251 *Id.* at 320.

government for outright grants of monopoly have no incentive for efficiency or customer service.[252]

Murphy is of the opinion that the government created the antitrust laws primarily to allow smaller rivals to attack more efficient competitors. Thus, he states that firms that lose in free competition are the ones that usually file antitrust suits. He notes that dominant firms are always subject to competition by new entrants to the market absent government protections and privileges granted to these large firms.

In this regard, Murphy believes that the government should not have broken up John D. Rockefeller's Standard Oil refinery business under the antitrust laws notwithstanding the fact that Standard Oil controlled 90 percent of the market after twenty years in that line of business.

He notes that Standard Oil achieved that dominance by forcing the price of kerosene down from 58 cents to 8 cents per gallon through reduction of costs (e.g., by producing its own oil barrels and hiring chemists to develop hundreds of byproducts from the refining process).

Murphy also notes that Standard Oil was able to cut costs because of shipping rebates from railroad companies because of efficiencies caused by bulk shipping. The rebates given to Standard Oil for its bulk shipping illustrates a concept known as "economies of scale." Economies of scale are present when long-run average costs fall as output expands. This results when a given increase in all inputs results in a more than proportional increase in output. Murphy's position is that free market mergers of competitors will only be profitable when they promote efficiency through economies of scale or some other mechanism.

In summary, Murphy views antitrust law as special interest legislation designed to allow smaller firms to gain an advantage over their more efficient competitors. Moreover, the goal of the antitrust laws is to protect competition, not competitors.[253]

---

252 *Id.* at 224.

253 *Id.* at 225–226. *See also* Brunswick Corp. v. Pueblo Bowl-O-Mat, 429 U.S. 477 (1977) (Congress enacted the antitrust laws to protect competition, not competitors).

Murphy's position focuses solely on the free market goal of achieving low cost for consumers. This is consistent with Robert Bork's 1978 thesis that he set forth in his book titled *The Antitrust Paradox*.[254] Bork's book changed the judicial approach from assuring fair competition to ensuring low cost for consumers.

However, Murphy's analysis seems to ignore the purpose of the antitrust laws to ensure fair competition and to limit overwhelming market power in one firm. Regulators in the Biden administration have shown a renewed focus on this aspect of the antitrust laws. In their view, dominant technology companies appear to be using their market power to engage in anticompetitive practices to crush competitors.[255] This is a continuation of the clash between the desire of persons and entities to be free of regulation, on one hand, and the role of the government to protect the greater interests of society generally on the other hand.

### 9. *Whether it is Wise for the Government to Enact Rent Control Laws?*

Murphy argues that rent controls encourage landlords to reduce their maintenance expenses and, ultimately, hurts the poor. He notes that when government makes housing artificially cheaper, it creates housing shortages in both the short run and the long run. In the short run, rent control causes landlords to rent out fewer apartments at the lower price while causing prospective tenants to choose renting over buying. Murphy also maintains that in the long run, investors will be reluctant to develop property to build apartments because the developer can only rent the apartments at below market prices.[256]

Rent control, according to Murphy, results in there being more people with cash than available rental units. As a result, Murphy maintains that

---

254 ROBERT H. BORK, THE ANTITRUST PARADOX (1978).
255 Lina Khan, *Amazon's Antitrust Paradox*, 126 Yale L.J. 710, 717 (2017), Amazon's Antitrust Paradox, The Yale Law Journal https://www.yalelawjournal.org › pdf › e.710.K....
256 *Id.* at 226.

minorities and disadvantaged groups will be hurt most as the landlord is likely to become choosier in determining to whom the landlord will rent.[257]

In this instance, Murphy does have empirical support for his thesis on rent control. Accordingly, it is debatable whether rent control as a remedy generally constitutes "smart" regulation.[258]

## 10. Whether the Government Should Have Enacted Minimum Wage Laws?

Murphy argues that minimum wage laws create unemployment. Without producing any statistics or studies, Murphy appears to assume that employers, instead of paying the minimum wage, will lay off workers and require that the employees who remain to become more productive. What Murphy is actually contending is that the free market should be the exclusive determinant of how much an employee should be paid. He categorically rejects any attempt by government to impose a floor on what a prospective employer must pay an employee no matter how low the government sets the minimum wage.[259]

This is consistent with neoliberalism's definition of liberty as individual freedom from government regulation, and the ability to organize relationships on the basis of free contracts between consenting adults.[260]

In this regard, he notes that if employers are paying their workers significantly less than what the workers add to their employer's bottom line of net profits—i.e., what economists refer to as the employee's marginal revenue product—other employers could earn significant profits by hiring away these

---

257 *Id.*

258 See Anthony Downs, *Residential Rent Controls: An Evaluation*, Urban Land Institute (1988), Residential Rent Controls University of California, Irvine https://www.socsci .uci.edu › ~jkbrueck › Downs

As a general rule, American economists have found that rent controls are neither an appropriate nor effective response to perceived housing shortages. In order for rent control to work, demand for rental units must rise sharply at the same time that new construction of such units that have been legally restricted. However, this does not typically occur.

259 ROGERS, *supra* note 11, at 227.

260 *Id.* at 17–18, 199–200.

underpaid workers at a slightly higher pay rate. In other words, in a free market system, purchasers pay a higher price for a scarce good or service and less for a good or service that is a dime a dozen.[261]

However, research indicates that the predictions of conservatives on the effects of minimum wage legislation do not mirror what happens in the real world. Indeed, when economists have analyzed the data, they have found few, if any, negative effects of the minimum wage on employment opportunities.[262]

## 11. Whether the Government Should Support Labor Unions?

Murphy maintains that unions reduce the incentives of employers to hire new workers. This results in employers failing to hire low-skilled workers who would otherwise receive training and move up the ranks. In contrast, capitalist investment in the free market increases employment and results in better working conditions. Murphy's thesis is that unions obtain benefits for their members through force and not as a result of the employer's voluntary cost-cutting measures or through the employees improved productivity as would occur in a truly free market.[263]

## 12. Whether the Government Should Have Enacted Safety Rules to Protect Workers and Consumers?

Murphy argues that market forces alone (i.e., the desire to make a profit and for repeat business) are sufficient to protect the safety of workers and consumers more than any regulatory laws. His position is that a firm's incentive to make profit will result in the firm's production of quality products and services in a safe way.[264]

---

261　*Id.*
262　*Id.* at 110–111.
263　*Id.* at 228.
264　*Id.* at 228.

Ironically, Murphy's thesis ultimately relies on a governmentally created and supported "framework of law and property rights" "where all contractual relationships are voluntary" and where courts "strictly enforce[] those rights." Accordingly, injured parties have the courts to enforce any wrongs perpetrated against them by their employers. Ultimately, however, Murphy grounds his thesis on the libertarian notion espoused by "classical liberals" that people should be free to choose whether to abide by government mandated safety requirements or to ignore them.

With respect to his opposition to governmentally imposed work-safety rules, Murphy first notes that in a competitive free market, employers pay their employees based on how much profit the employees make for their firms. Murphy then argues that government imposed workplace safety standards are inefficient because the costs to employers in implementing these mechanisms are costly and result in lower employee compensation. **In his view, workers should be allowed to take their chances at getting injured on the job in exchange for a higher paycheck.**[265]

Similarly, Mr. Murphy notes the Food and Drug Administration has enacted policies that make it almost prohibitively expensive for pharmaceutical companies to develop new drugs. As a result, these government policies have stifled the creation of new and innovative drugs. With respect to government mandated seat belt laws, he notes that these laws, though well intended, have had the unintended consequence of increasing non-fatal accidents. Murphy appears to infer that these crash survivors become a burden on society and that society would be better off if these persons died from their injuries.[266]

Similarly, while Murphy concedes that government mandated air bags in cars may prevent deaths in severe accidents, he also cites a study that indicates that they are inherently dangerous and have had the unintended consequence of increasing the likelihood of death in lower speed crashes.

Murphy notes that under the **law of unintended consequences**, when the government attempts to solve problems by coercion, their will inevitably be

---

265 *Id.* at 228–229.
266 *Id.* at 229.

unforeseen consequences. For example, he notes that "[w]*elfare benefits* may encourage out-of-wedlock births" which results in an "increase in poverty and crime"; "*rent control* may make it difficult for the poor to find decent housing"; "*laws requiring child-resistant packaging* for medicine may cause the elderly to store pills in unmarked containers, leading to more overdoses"; and that *curfews* may reduce the rate of petty crime while increasing the rate of violent crimes.[267]

According to Murphy, this is because curfews reduce the amount of places police can be at one time and also reduce a considerable number of eyewitnesses from the streets at night.

Murphy is in favor of what he refers to as "free market protection" instead of governmentally imposed safety rules. He cites as examples of "free market protection" MasterCard and Visa's chargeback procedures which protect consumers from fraud; privately enforced rules and standards which provide oversight and private regulation such as Underwriters Laboratories, ratings agencies such as Moody's; and rules and standards imposed by private insurance companies as a prerequisite for issuing a liability policy.[268]

## 13. Whether it is Wise for the Government to Enact Occupational Licensing Laws?

Murphy again argues that market forces (i.e., the desire to make a profit and for repeat business) protect consumers more than any regulatory laws. He states that these market forces make it unnecessary for governments to impose licensing standards on professionals or any other government-imposed safety standard. For example, Murphy states that government mandated licensing of physicians: (1) raises the costs of medical services; (2) is more concerned with stifling competition by non-licensed care givers than protecting patients; (3) results in less medical care to members of the public because there are fewer care givers to provide medical services; (4) "stifles research efforts in

---

267  *Id.* at 229.
268  *Id.* at 229–230.

unapproved areas"; and (5) causes "doctors to waste time performing routine medical procedures that . . . could be handled by nurses." Additionally, Murphy states that "The American Medical Association is a cartel that raises medical costs.[269]

Murphy's analysis does not seem to strike a proper balance between the desire of persons to be free from government regulation and the need to protect society. Indeed, in some instances, legislatures and courts have determined that the government has overregulated or should not have regulated certain occupations.[270]Accordingly, in the area of occupational licensing, the challenge on government is to enact "smart" regulation. But a categorical rule opposed to any government power to license occupations would be an abdication of the government's role to protect the public health, safety, and welfare.

## 14. Whether Cryptocurrency Should be Regulated?

### a. Bitcoin as the Libertarian's Dream of Life Without Government Regulation

The Bitcoin idea is the libertarian's dream of life without government regulation.[271] "The thinking was that the global financial system was creaky and controlled by sclerotic governments. A new system based on a decentralized accounting technology called blockchain would democratize the worldwide exchange of goods and services.[272]

---

269 *Id.* at 230.

270 W. Sherman Rogers, *Occupational Licensing: Quality Control or Enterprise Killer? Problems that Arise When People Must Get the Government's Permission to Work*, 10 J. Bus. Entrepreneurship & L. 145 (2017).
*Available at:* https://digitalcommons.pepperdine.edu/jbel/vol10/iss2/1.

271 Matt O' Brien, *Bitcoin Shows What Libertarians Get Wrong About Money*, WASH. POST, January16, 2018, sec.A12, Bitcoin is teaching libertarians everything they don't know ...https://www.washingtonpost.com › wonk › 2018/01/08.

272 Adam Lashinsky, *Crypto is a Solution in Search of a Problem*, WASH. POST, May 22, 2022, at A27, Opinion Crypto is a solution in search of a problem *Washington Post* https://www.washingtonpost.com › 2022/05/20 › cryp...

In practice, however, cryptocurrencies aren't used as actual currency to pay for anything except pornography and criminal activity. Even Coinbase, a large crypto-exchange charges its customers in dollars.[273] The reality is that most Americans buy cryptocurrency as a speculative investment, not as a way to pay for goods and services. Moreover, there is little to indicate that this will change.[274]

And, now, in view of the colossal collapse of the FTX cryptocurrency exchange in December 2022, there are mounting calls for the regulation of cryptocurrencies.[275] But, first, let's discuss why some believe that bitcoin and other cryptocurrencies fail as both a medium of exchange and as a store of value.

### b. Do Bitcoin and Other Cryptocurrencies Fail as a Medium of Exchange?

According to columnist Matt O' Brien, **Bitcoin can handle only a maximum of 7 transactions per second while Visa can handle 56,000 transactions per second.** Therefore, he maintains that Bitcoin largely fails as a medium of exchange in today's world economy.[276]

**The type of computers necessary to solve bitcoins cryptographically complex equations consume more than 0.1 percent of all the world's electricity (about as much as Denmark does)** which is remarkable when you consider how little bitcoin is currently used. And a lot of these computers

---

273 *Id.*

274 Tony Newmyer, *Cryptocurrency Everywhere—Except in the Cash Register*, WASH. POST, January 12, 2022, A14, Cryptocurrency is suddenly everywhere *Washington Post* https://www.washingtonpost.com › crypto-versus-cash.

275 Allison Verspille, Lydia Beyoud, *Bring on the Crypto Regulators: If FTX Had Followed Existing U.S. Rules, Many Customers Would Have Been Protected and it May Not Have Imploded,* Bloomberg Businessweek, December 12, 2022, at 20–21; Paul Kiernan, *FTX's Fall Halts Push for Light Oversight*, Wall St. J., November 28, 2022, at 23, FTX's Fall Halts Push For Light Oversight PressReader.com https://www.pressreader.com › usa › the-wall-street-journal.

276 Matt O' Brien, *supra* note 271.

still rely on dirty coal as the source of the energy they need to perform the necessary verification transactions.[277]

Bitcoin's strictly limited money supply—21 million and no more—harks back to a time when money was a shiny rock you dug out of the ground, not a piece of paper we call currency that we also use as a medium of exchange. Bitcoin's limited supply is why bitcoin's price went from being able to buy $900.00 worth of things one year to $19,000 the next year. When this happens, owners of bitcoin stop using it to purchase things and wait to become bitcoin millionaires.[278]

The point of all of this is to illustrate the fact that money is not only a store of value but also a medium of exchange. Accordingly, if bitcoin ever replaced the dollar, it would bring the world economy to a halt because it would be hoarded as a store of value like gold and would not be used as a medium of exchange. Accordingly, the liquidity of bitcoin is questionable for these very reasons, among others.

### c. Do Bitcoin and Other Cryptocurrencies Fail as a Store of Value?

To keep people from hoarding dollars as primarily a store of value, on the other hand, the Federal Reserve can increase the supply of dollars when demand grows for dollars and decrease the supply of dollars when demand decreases.[279]

Increases in the money supply by the Fed ultimately decreases interest rates and keeps the value of currency stable in light of current economic conditions. On the other hand, decreases in the money supply by the Fed ultimately increases interest rates while keeping the value of the currency stable in light of current economic conditions.[280]

---

277 Chris Mooney, Steven Mufson, Why the Bitcoin Craze is Using Up So Much Energy—
WASH. POST, December 17, 2017), https://www.washingtonpost.com/news/energy-environment/wp/2017/12/19/why-the-bitcoin-craze-is-using-up-so-much-energy/?utm_term=.0e3c7f8610f0 (December 19, 2017); Matt O' Brien, *supra* note 271.
278 Matt O' Brien, *supra* note 271.
279 *Id.*
280 ROGERS, *supra* note 11, at 265–270.

The Fed increases or decreases the money supply through its Federal Open Market Committee. It accomplishes this result by deciding daily whether to buy government bonds from designated primary dealers (which increases the money supply) or selling government bonds to these designated primary dealers (which decreases the money supply). Primary dealers serve as counterparties of the New York Fed in its implementation of monetary policy.[281]

However, there is no central organization like the Federal Open Market Committee to increase or decrease the supply of bitcoin. Accordingly, bitcoin—whose units cannot be increased or decreased—will continue to have wild swings in value that will make it more of an investment as opposed to a medium of exchange at any given moment.[282]

Nobel Prize winning Economist Paul Krugman is a major crypto skeptic for two reasons: (1) high transaction costs and (2) the absence of any tethering. The dollar is backstopped by the fact that the U.S. government will accept dollars as payment for taxes—liabilities it is able to enforce because it is a government.

Cryptocurrencies, Krugman maintains, have no backstop, no tether to reality. He also maintains that, instead of money created by a click of a mouse, cryptocurrencies involve money that must be mined—i.e., created through resource intensive computations. In Krugman's view, "crypto currency enthusiasts are effectively celebrating the use of cutting-edge technology to set the monetary system back three hundred years."[283]

Money is an asset that serves as a medium of exchange with which people buy and sell goods. "Coins, currency (such as dollar bills), and checking accounts all serve as money." An asset, in turn, is physical property or an intangible right that has economic value. Using money for trade eliminates the need of people to seek a double coincidence of wants, as is true in the case of barter. . . . On the other hand, money is not savings, income, or borrowings; these are all real

---

281  *Id.* at 263–270.

282  Matt O' Brien, *supra* note 271.

283  PAUL KRUGMAN, ARGUING WITH ZOMBIES: ECONOMICS, POLITICS, AND THE FIGHT FOR A BETTER FUTURE 411–414 (2020), reproducing one of his New York Times Columns titled: *Transaction Costs and Tethers: Why I'm a Crypton-Skeptic,* July 31, 2018.

physical goods and services. For example, income is the real goods and services that a person earns. Therefore, just as a picture of a house is not the house, ***money is only a measure of the value of a goods and services***; it is not the goods and services themselves.[284] For all the reasons earlier mentioned, Bitcoin and other cryptocurrencies also fail miserably as a measure of the value of goods and services.

An asset is liquid if it can be easily traded for goods and services without taking a loss. Money is the most liquid asset. Bitcoin fails this test. As one commentator noted, "Bitcoin changes prices too quickly to be currency and processes transactions too slowly to be a payments system.[285]

### d. The Collapse of FTX and Calls for the Regulation of Cryptocurrency

The Collapse of FTX, a major cryptocurrency exchange, exposed the dangers of this unregulated system.[286] Among other things, FTX (1) **comingled customers funds** with its own[287]; (2) **did not have any obligation to register its panoply of separate business lines** with the respective regulator as would be required for regulated firms[288]; (3) **failed to disclose material information** about risks[289]; (4) used celebrities to advertise the FTX platform without

---

284 ROGERS, *supra* note 11, at 271.

285 Matt O' Brien, *supra* note 271.

286 Allyson Versprille and Lydia Beyoud, *supra* note 275, at 20.

287 *Id.* FTX failed to protect its customers assets by lending customer funds to its sister company, hedge fund Alameda Research, to shore up risky trades. FTX and other crypto exchanges claim that crypto tokens are not securities regulated by the Securities and Exchange Commission. Additionally, the Commodities Futures Trading Commission has no current congressional authority to regulate crypto commodities.

288 *Id.* FTX's platforms, like other crypto exchanges, performed many functions including market making, trading, custodianship and securities lending. By contrast, traditional financial firms that provide different financial services usually register their separate business lines with the respective regulators.

289 *Id.* at 20–21. The SEC already has rules that stops individuals from touting securities without disclosing payment details. But actions against celebrity endorsers depends on whether the SEC and others consider crypto tokens to be securities. The SEC used its purported authority in such matters to fine Kim Kardashian. Ms. Kardashian paid a $1.26 million fine without admitting or denying liability. *See* SEC Charges Kim Kardashian for Unlawfully Touting Crypto . . . https://www.sec.gov › news › press-release › 2022–183.

disclosing the details about payment to these celebrities; and (5) did not have any **internal controls** to prevent wrongdoing or any **other corporate governance standards** as required for publicly traded companies.[290]

In light of this, one commentator concluded that "Congress and financial regulators may need to tweak existing rules to cover the crypto industry, but a brand-new set of crypto-specific authorities may not be needed.[291]

## 15. Whether Prohibitions Against Insider Trading of Securities be Abolished?

It is a well-established rule of law that any person in possession of material nonpublic information about a security must either disclose it to the investing public or abstain from trading or recommending the security while inside information about the security remains undisclosed. This is because of the inherent unfairness involved when a party takes advantage of the information knowing that it is unavailable to those with whom he is dealing.[292]

When insider trading takes place, it allows the well-connected to profit from privileged information. The law takes the position that these insiders should not be able to profit at the expense of ordinary people who lack this undisclosed information. But some libertarians and neoliberal scholars believe

---

290 *Id.* at 21. FTX's new, post-bankruptcy CEO, John Ray III, told the bankruptcy court not to trust FTX's financial statements and that most of FTX entities never held board meetings. The Sarbanes-Oxley Act, enacted after the fall of Enron Corporation, requires internal control checks on audits done on publicly held companies but not for closely held firms. *See* Alexander Saeedy, Soma Biswas, Eliot Brown, *New CEO Says FTX Fiasco Is Without Precedent: Unaudited Statements, Absence of Records Led to Abuses at Crypto Platform Filing Says*, Wall St. J., November 18, 2022, at 81, Alexander Saeedy, Soma Biswas, FTX's New CEO Faults Lax Oversight in Bankruptcy Filing Wall Street Journal https://www.wsj.com › articles › ftxs-new-chief-says-com...

291 Allyson Versprille, *supra* note 275, at 21.

292 In the Matter of Cady Roberts & Co., 40 S.E.C. 907, 911–912 (1961); SEC v. Texas Gulph Sulphur Co., 833 F. 2d. 833 (2d Cir. 1968), *cert. denied*, 404 U.S. 1005 (1971). The United States Supreme Court has repeatedly affirmed this rule. *See, e.g.,* United States v. O'Hagan, 521 U.S. 642 (1997); Dirks v. SEC, 463 U.S. 646 (1983).

that insider trading is good and *should not be prohibited* because it helps to disseminate information more quickly, making markets more efficient.[293]

Libertarianism is a type of anti-statism—a term that describes opposition to government intervention (i.e., intervention by "the state") into personal, social, and economic affairs. Libertarians believe that any government activity that extends beyond protection of people from violence, theft, or enforcing contracts is illegitimate. Overall, libertarians believe that America should be governed by individual liberty, a peaceful foreign policy, minimal government, and a free market economy.[294]

Libertarians base their arguments in favor of legalizing insider trading on the efficient market hypothesis. This theory posits that a stock's current price accurately reflects all the information an investor can possibly know about the stock.[295] The efficient market hypothesis, when used in this manner, appears to be consistent with lassiez-faire, liberty-based theories to avoid regulation.

Libertarians and like-minded persons *analogize their belief that lawmakers should legalize insider trading to their similar belief in the legalization of drugs. In their opinion, the government would be released from the burden of fighting an expensive losing battle.*[296]

Libertarians argue that markets detect the presence of an informed purchaser or seller of a company's stock. Therefore, those in favor of legalization of insider trading *predict* that when an insider *buys* stock in a company based on material nonpublic information, the market will (or should) detect the presence of an informed buyer and cause the stock of the company to go up. On the other hand, they *predict* that when an insider *sells* stock in a company based on material nonpublic information, the market will (or should) detect

---

293 Liam Vaughan, *Is it Luck or Insider Trading,* Bloomberg BusinessWeek, October 4, 2021, at 47, Is Stock Market Rigged? Insider Trading by Executives Is ...Bloomberghttps://www.bloomberg.com › news › features › is-sto.

294 ROGERS, *supra* note 11, at 54–55.

295 VIRGINIA MORRIS, KENNETH M. MORRIS, STANDARD & POOR'S GUIDE TO MONEY AND INVESTING 103 (2006).

296 Liam Vaughan, *supra* note 293, at 47.

the presence of an informed seller and cause the stock of the company to go down.[297]

Indeed, some opponents of laws prohibiting insider trading maintain that insider trading always pushes the price of stock in the correct direction. They maintain that trading volume, and other trade-specific characteristics such as trade size, direction, and frequency, *signal the presence of an informed trader in the market*. Accordingly, they maintain that government laws that prohibit insider trading are unnecessary. Indeed, the opponents believe that insider trading is beneficial.[298]

However, other commentators and scholars have produced studies that indicate that capital markets are not fundamentally efficient and do not always incorporate information into market prices. Professor David Rosenfeld's article demonstrates this—in the context of insider trading—through a series of compelling insider trading cases. Collectively, these cases indicate that buying and selling by an informed [insider] trader are often not reflected in the market price of the stock. Indeed, in some instances, the insider's trades caused the market price to go in a direction that is opposite of what efficient market advocates predict.[299]

Those who favor prohibitions against insider trading argue that long-term market integrity is more important than any possible short-term market efficiency. In their view, it seems unfair to allow insiders to take advantage of information that is not equally available to other participants.[300]

*In cases involving an inside trader who trades on undisclosed material information regarding **good news** about a company*, the inside trader *buys* shares of stock in the business while outside shareholders who do not possess the information sell their shares. When the business officially reveals the good

---

297 David Rosenfeld, *The Impact of Insider Trading on the Market Price of Securities: Some Evidence From Recent Cases of Unlawful Trading*, 44:1 J. Corp. L. 65, 67 (2018), "The Impact of Insider Trading on the Market Price of Securities ...Northern Illinois Universityhttps://huskiecommons.lib.niu.edu › clglaw › clglaw.

298 *Id.*

299 *Id.*

300 *Id.* at 68.

news, the stock price goes up even higher and the insider profits on the difference between the lower purchase price and the subsequent higher price. The inside trader can also achieve the same result by purchasing call options on the company's stock.

On the other hand, *in cases involving an insider who trades on undisclosed material information regarding* **bad news** *about a company,* the inside trader *sells* shares of stock in the company while those without the information continue to purchase the shares in the corporation. When the business officially reveals the bad news, the stock price goes down and the insider profits on the difference between the higher sales price and the subsequent lower price. Insiders accomplish this result by borrowing the company's stock from a broker and selling the borrowed stock short at today's prices. When the price of the stock goes down after the announcement of the bad news, the insider trader repurchases the borrowed shares at the lower price and returns the stock to the broker. Insiders can also achieve the same result by purchasing put options on the company's stock.

The opponents of insider trading laws believe that insiders who trade on undisclosed material information do no harm to traders who lack that information. And some, as stated earlier, take the position that insider trading can even be beneficial. *They state that this is because the markets detect an informed trader's presence in the market* and that a large portion of the insider's trading is reflected in the market price of the stock prior to the public disclosure of the information.[301]

Accordingly, the opponents of insider trading prohibitions argue that when an insider *buys* shares of stock in a company based on material undisclosed *good news* about the company, *this causes the market price of the firm's stock to go up.* Conversely, they argue that when an insider *sells* shares of stock in a company based on undisclosed *bad news* about a company, *this causes the market price of the firm's stock to go down.*

However, Rosenfeld's article carefully analyzes a group of "recent cases of known insider trading . . . [,] . . . where the market fail[ed] to detect the

---

301  *Id.* at 69.

presence of informed traders, and even instances where stock prices move[d] in the contrary direction." Indeed, in some cases, an insider's *significant purchases* of a company's stock based on material undisclosed *good news* about the company did not cause the company's stock to rise as expected and, in some cases, the company's stock even dropped in price.[302]

Rosenfeld also cites cases in which an insider's *significant sales* of a company's stock based on material undisclosed *bad news* about a company did not cause the company's stock to fall as expected and, in some cases, even witnessed a rise in the company's stock prices.[303]

Rosenfeld's article, while not dismissive of the efficient market hypothesis in the context of insider trading, points to several important insider trading cases that cast serious doubt on the theory. Indeed, *Rosenfeld's article painstakingly demonstrates many instances in which an insider's trades did not actually* affect the market price of a company's stock in the manner predicted by proponents of efficient market theory. Interestingly, some have argued that overwhelming empirical evidence now suggests that capital markets are not fundamentally efficient.[304]

### 16. Whether it is Appropriate for the Government to Regulate the Business Model of Uber, Lyft, and other Gig Economy Companies?

The sharing economy (sometimes referred to as the Gig Economy or the online platform economy) seeks out independent contractors to provide services to customers. Gig economy platforms such as Uber emphasize that contractors have the benefits of "[f]lexible hours, being [their] own boss, [and] the glories and self-bootstrapping pride of entrepreneurship." "These are among

---

302  *Id.* at 69–70, 75–77.
303  *Id.* at 77–79.
304  *See* Halliburton Co. v. Erica P. John Fund, Inc., 573 U.S. 258 (2014) (argument of Haliburton Co.).

the virtues of 'sharing economy' gigs, as touted in an Uber-commissioned survey of its drivers."[305]

Other companies offering peer-to-peer platforms such as Airbnb, TaskRabbit and Homejoy, have made similar pitches: "They're giving workers—particularly those who are unable to land traditional jobs or unfulfilled by 9–5 Organization Man duties—the freedom to take their breadwinning fates into their own hands."[306] Indeed, it is clear that the gig economy has created income opportunities for many people who, otherwise, might find it difficult to find employment.

The risk, however, according to one commentator, is that entrepreneurs involved in most sharing economy gigs—who provide services as independent contractors—do not have access to traditional corporate safety net programs administered by employers such as health insurance, workers compensation, and a variety of other benefits available only to employees but not to independent contractors.[307] Some historians refer to these traditional corporate safety net programs as welfare capitalism.

A lot hinges on whether the law classifies a worker as an employee or an independent contractor. If a court determines that the law requires an employer to classify a worker as an employee under the relevant legal standard, the employer must provide the worker with several state and federal benefits for which the worker would not otherwise be eligible.

On the other hand, a determination that a worker is an independent contractor means that the worker will not receive those protections and benefits. Historically, in determining whether a worker is an independent contractor or an employee, courts have focused on whether the employer has the right to control the manner, method, and details about how the worker performs

---

305 *See* Catherine Rampell, *The Dark Side of the Sharing Economy*, WASH. POST, January 27, 2015, at A17, The dark side of 'sharing economy' jobs *Washington Post* https://www.washingtonpost.com › 2015/01/26.
306 *Id.*
307 *Id.*

his or her work. If a court finds the requisite control, the court will deem the worker to be an employee.[308]

In this context, the sharing economy looks more like a continuation of the disintegration of the corporation-centered safety net—e.g., the disappearance of defined benefit pension plans, increased use of temporary workers, as well as just-in-time scheduling, and outsourcing.

In view of this, California decided that it needed to protect gig workers. Accordingly, California passed legislation in 2019 that transformed Uber, Lyft, Postmates, Door Dash, Instacart, and other app-based business contractors into putative employees. The legislation secured for these contractors and other app-based businesses, benefits such as the minimum wage, paid sick days, and worker's compensation benefits.[309]

However, critics of the California legislation widely complained that the bill was paternalistic, and created unintended consequences because some groups of freelance drivers enjoyed complete control over their work schedule.[310] Moreover, ride sharing and delivery companies feared that the California legislation might cause their business models to fail.

Consequently, a group of app-based ride sharing and delivery companies successfully initiated a voter referendum known as Proposition 22 that: (1) nullified the California legislation, but only for rideshare and delivery

---

308 A full-blown discussion of the various standards that the law uses, in different contexts, to determine whether a worker is an employee, or an independent contractor is beyond the scope of this book. In any case, if the courts determine that a person is an independent contractor, that person has no rights under the Age Discrimination in Employment Act; Title VII of the 1964 Civil Rights Act; the Fair Labor Standards Act; Workers Compensation Statutes; employer benefits intended only for "employees"; and a host of other protections and benefits. *See* ALFRED F. CONARD, ROBERT L. KNAUSS, STANLEY SIEGEL, AGENCY-PARTNERSHIPS 157–180. *See also* Employee Versus Independent Contractor—Digital Media Law ...https://www.dmlp .org › legal-guide › employee-versus-... ; Patrick G. Brady, Julie Saker Schlegel, Trump Administration's DOL Rejects Obama-Era Guidance on ...wagehourblog.com https:// www.wagehourblog.com › FLSA Coverage; Kristin Downey Grimsley, *Revenge of the Temps: Independent Contractors' Victory in Microsoft Case May Have Wide Impact*, WASH. POST, January 16, 2000, at H1.

309 Caroline O'Donovan, *Uber and Lyft Spend Hundreds of Millions to Win Their Fight Over Workers' Rights. It Worked.* www.buzzfeednews.com/article/carolineodonovan/...

310 *Id.*

companies; (2) restored their workers' status as independent contractors; and (3) provided workers with minimum earnings, health-care subsidies, and occupational accident insurance.[311]

A September 2018 report by JP Morgan Chase Institute found that a majority of people who earn full time income from the "online platform economy" only sporadically utilize these opportunities to earn income as independent contractors. The report found that an increasing number of these part-time entrepreneurs were using gig economy work to supplement a 9–5 job.[312] Therefore, this suggests that legislation intended to help gig workers may, indeed, be paternalistic and have the unintended consequence of taking away some of the unfettered freedom that they previously enjoyed.

Statistics vary on whether drivers believe they have benefitted from maintaining their independent contractor status. However, one study by Benson Strategy Group found that 77 percent of drivers believed that they had benefitted from Proposition 22. And it appears that most gig workers prefer independent contractor status with some minimal benefits.[313]

Interestingly, the Biden administration is proposing a new federal rule that could put more gig workers on companies payrolls as employees. The rule would scrap a Trump administration rule that made it easier for firms to classify workers as independent contractors. Under federal labor law, employees are eligible for protections such as the minimum wage, medical leave, and overtime pay that don't apply to independent contractors.[314]

---

311 Maeve Allsup, *Gig Companies Face California Crackdowns That Uber, Lyft Escape,* Gig Companies Face California Crackdowns That Uber, Lyft ...bloomberglaw.com https://news.bloomberglaw.com › daily-labor-report.

312 Jenna McGregor, *'Gig Economy' Not a 9–5 Replacement,* WASH. POST, September 25, 2018, at A14, How much people really make in the 'gig economy' *Washington Post* https://www.washingtonpost.com › 2018/09/24 › how..
The JP Morgan Chase Institute refers to the gig/sharing economy as the "online platform economy."

313 Brian Straight, Do gig workers want to be employees? It depends who you ...FreightWaves https://www.freightwaves.com › news › do-gig-worke...

314 Gabriel T. Rubin, David Harrison, Proposal Aims to Regulate Gig Workers, Wall St. J. October 12, 2022, A1.
Biden Rule Would Add More Gig Workers to Company ...https://www.wsj.com › articles › labor-department-pro...

Arguably, the proposed Biden rule constitutes government interference in the ability of companies to organize their relationships with their workers on the basis of free contracts between consenting adults. Moreover, if most gig workers want the freedom to work or not to work as they please without any control over their time, they may view the proposed rule as a paternalistic effort with unintended negative consequences. As conservative economist Robert P. Murphy would undoubtedly say, "when government intervenes in the market, it not only tramples on freedom, and individual rights, but it also often hurts the very people it presumes to help."[315]

## 17. Whether the Government Should Regulate the Development and Use of Artificial Intelligence (Face Recognition, Algorithms, etc.) That Create Racial and Other Effects?

### a. What Is Artificial Intelligence?

Algorithms lie at the heart of artificial intelligence and machine learning. And, as we shall see, algorithms duplicate the biases of their creators.

Artificial intelligence is a poorly defined term, which contributes to the confusion between it and machine learning, says Bethany Edmunds, associate dean and lead faculty for Northeastern University's computer science master's program.[316]

"Artificial intelligence is essentially a system that seems smart. That's not a very good definition, though, because it's like saying that something is 'healthy.' What exactly does that mean?" she says. "On a basic level, artificial intelligence is where a machine seems human-like and can imitate human behavior."[317]

---

315 ROGERS, *supra* note 11, at 216.
316 Artificial Intelligence vs. Machine Learning: What's the Difference?
Northeastern University Graduate Programs › graduate › blog › artificial-intelligence
-vs-machin...
317 *Id.*

These behaviors include problem-solving, learning, and planning, for example, which are achieved through analyzing data and identifying patterns within it in order to replicate those behaviors.

## b. What Is Machine Learning?

Machine learning (ML), on the other hand, is a type of artificial intelligence, Edmunds says. "Where artificial intelligence is the overall appearance of being smart, machine learning is where machines are taking in data and learning things about the world that would be difficult for humans to do," she says. "ML can go beyond human intelligence."[318]

ML is primarily used to process large quantities of data very quickly using algorithms that change over time and get better at what they're intended to do. A manufacturing plant might collect data from machines and sensors on its network in quantities far beyond what any human is capable of processing. ML is then used to spot patterns and identify anomalies, which may indicate a problem that humans can then address.

"Machine learning is a technique that allows machines to get information that humans can't," she says. "We don't really know how our vision or language systems work—it's difficult to articulate in an easy way. For this reason, we're relying on data and feeding it to computers so they can simulate what they think we're doing. That's what machine learning does."

And quantum machines will speed up the process. Google, for example, said its quantum computer took less than three and half minutes to perform a calculation that would take the most powerful classical computer on the planet 10,000 years to compute.[319]

---

318 *Id.*

319 Jeanne Whalen, *Amazon Joins Race for Quantum Tech With Caltech Center,* WASH. POST, October 27, 2021, at A18, Amazon joins race for quantum computer with new Caltech ...*Washington Post*
https://www.washingtonpost.com › 2021/10/26 › ama...

### c. Algorithmic Bias

Ironically, the first instance of algorithmic bias began with Dr. Geoffrey Franglen's idea of creating a fairer and more efficient admissions process.[320] As an assessor, Dr. Franglen evaluated candidates seeking admission to St. George's Hospital Medical School.[321] Due to the large volume of applications the school received each year, Dr. Franglen sought a more efficient process.[322] In response, he wrote an algorithm to mirror the assessors' considerations when deciding between applicants.[323] Before entirely relying on the algorithm, the assessors used their traditional evaluation process and the algorithm to evaluate the candidates.[324]

In 1979, the human assessors and the algorithm saw similar results in 90 to 95 percent of cases.[325] By 1982, the school relied on the algorithm entirely to evaluate the school's candidates. Dr. Franglen designed the algorithm to sort through thousands of applicants fairly and efficiently.[326] However, this process was anything but fair. After relying on the algorithm altogether, applicants complained that the students the algorithm chose were not diverse.[327] A U.K. investigatory body opened an examination of the medical school's evaluation process, and it determined that the algorithm was discriminatory against women and non-European applicants.[328]

---

320 Oscar Schwartz, *Untold History of AI: Algorithmic Bias Was Born in the 1980s*, IEEE Spectrum (Apr. 15, 2019), https://spectrum.ieee.org/tech-talk/tech-history/dawn-of-electronics/untold-history-of-ai-the-birth-of-machine-bias; *Algorithmic bias was born 40 years ago*, ThinkAutomation (last visited Apr. 30, 2021), https://www.thinkautomation.com/automation-ethics/algorithmic-bias-was-born-40-years-ago/#:~:text=Biases%20and%20discrimination%20are%20issues,should%20be%20immune%20to%20bias.&text=In%20fact%2C%20the%20issue%20of,a%20whole%20four%20decades%20ago..

321 *Id.*

322 *Id.*

323 *Id.*

324 *Id.*

325 *Id.*

326 *Id.*

327 *Id.*

328 *Id.*

The similarity between the selected candidates through the manual evaluation process and via the algorithm begs the question: Can an algorithm be biased? Why was the school not investigated for bias in years past for choosing a similar class of students? The following discussion will briefly answer these questions by providing a definition of an algorithm.

While they may seem like cutting-edge and complex mechanisms, algorithms are quite simple and have been used by many people, in their daily lives, for centuries. **In simple terms, an algorithm is "a set of instructions designed to perform a specific task."[329] According to this definition, baking a cake, laundry, and long division are all examples of algorithms that people perform daily.**[330] The more complex and sophisticated algorithms that tech companies utilize in our lives are still the same as the basic examples mentioned earlier; **however, complex algorithms are usually "a set of instructions telling a computer what to do and how to do it."**[331] The difference between these two definitions is the use of the computer. The use of a computer only changes the efficiency of performing tasks.

When considering both definitions of an algorithm, it becomes clear why bias is prevalent in algorithms. Computers follow the command of those who create the algorithm. Thus, if human-created algorithms command a computer to produce a specific result, the result will mirror what was envisioned in the human's mind, meaning that the results will include that human's biases. As a result, the computer's power and efficiency amplify the algorithm's creator's bias.

The use of an algorithm is likely why the U.K. investigatory body investigated the school's evaluation process despite the prior admissions system

---

329 *Algorithm*, Tech Terms, https://techterms.com/definition/algorithm (last visited Apr. 30, 2021).

330 *What Are Algorithms? A Guide to Algorithms for Children*, Juni Learning (Sept. 2, 2019), https://junilearning.com/blog/guide/what-are-algorithms/#:~:text=An%20algorithm%20is%20a%20set,or%20solving%20a%20particular%20problem.&text=The%20recipe%20for%20baking%20a,all%20examples%20of%20an%20algorithm.

331 Jacob Brogan, *Your Algorithms Cheat Sheet*, Slate (Feb. 2, 2016, 10:28 AM), https://slate.com/technology/2016/02/algorithms-101-a-cheat-sheet-to-the-terminology-the-ethical-debates-and-more.html.

producing similar results in the past. The use of an algorithm created a more efficient process to produce bias without human interference. Without human interference, an algorithm itself cannot detect a lack of diversity.

The algorithm used in the St. George's Hospital admission process demonstrates the idea that algorithms are not inherently biased or problematic. The problem of algorithmic bias is a human one. Therefore, the solution to algorithmic bias should not center on fixing an algorithm itself. Instead, the solution should be human-centered. The solution of algorithmic bias cannot be centered around changing algorithms because the harsh reality is that no matter how often the algorithm is tweaked to be more equitable, the goal of equity will never be reached. After all, algorithm creators use algorithms, whether consciously or unconsciously, as a tool to reinforce their ideas and opinions.

Data by itself is not of much value, but when it is analyzed and put into the context of a businesses' goals, data is invaluable.[332] Specifically, data can serve as the basis for corporate and government decisions.[333] Corporations use algorithms to collect masses of data from various sources. Corporations then use this data to profile their consumers' habits and preferences.[334] Examining the habits and preferences of consumers can help guide their decision-making on how to sell their products to their consumers.[335]

Algorithms can be useful for effectively and efficiently reaching outcomes that would take much more time for a human to reach.[336] Because of the convenience of algorithms, governments and corporations have increasingly relied on algorithms to make important decisions.[337] Since these outcomes are not achieved by a human, it would seem to follow that the computer's

---

332 *Id.*

333 *Id.*

334 Yeshimabeit Milner & Amy Traub, *Data Capitalism and Algorithmic Racism*, 6, https://www.demos.org/research/data-capitalism-and-algorithmic-racism (2021).

335 *Id.*

336 Salim Ismail, *Why Algorithms Are The Future of Business Success*, Growth Institute (last visited Nov. 23, 2021), https://blog.growthinstitute.com/exo/algorithms.

337 *Id.*

outcomes would be free of human error and bias. However, this is not true. Research suggests that algorithms actually perpetuate human bias on a greater level.

In the housing industry, marginalized communities are having harder times applying for housing and obtaining fair prices for loans due to the algorithms upon which they rely.[338] Similarly, in the job market, companies' use of algorithms are resulting in less diverse workforces.[339] On social media, where many people are making a living by uploading content, algorithms disfavor Black content creators, which significantly lowers their economic opportunities.[340]

The phenomenon of algorithms diminishing the economic opportunity of marginalized communities while benefiting powerful corporations is a part of *data capitalism*.[341] Scholars define data capitalism as "an economic model built on the extraction and commodification of data and the use of big data and algorithms as tools to concentrate and consolidate power in ways that dramatically increase inequality along lines of race, class, gender, and disability."[342] Basically, corporations treat data as a commodity that has great economic value. Corporations and governing institutions hoard and collect data to inform them of trends and behaviors that will largely influence their decision-making to reach their goal of being more profitable. Corporations work to achieve this goal even at the expense of marginalized communities' economic well-being.

---

338 *See* Patrick Sisson, *Housing discrimination goes high tech*, Curbed (Dec. 17, 2019, 6:12PM EST), https://archive.curbed.com/2019/12/17/21026311/mortgage-apartment-housing-algorithm-discrimination.

339 The Greenlining Institute, ALGORITHMIC BIAS EXPLAINED: HOW AUTOMATED DECISION-MAKING BECOMES AUTOMATED DISCRIMINATION, 19, https://greenlining.org/wp-content/uploads/2021/04/Greenlining-Institute-Algorithmic-Bias-Explained-Report-Feb-2021.pdf.

340 Janice Gassam Asare, *Does TikTok Have A Race Problem?*, Forbes (Apr. 14, 2020, 12:42 AM), https://www.forbes.com/sites/janicegassam/2020/04/14/does-tiktok-have-a-race-problem/?sh=7ae3ed1c3260.

341 Yeshimabeit Milner & Amy Traub, *Data Capitalism and Algorithmic Racism, supra* note 334.

342 *Id.*

Whether it be social media, the job market, or housing, algorithms have the power to economically affect marginalized communities with greater efficiency and effectiveness than a human.

### d. Steven Hawking's Warning About Artificial Intelligence

The late Stephen Hawking was well-known for his work on black holes and the theory of relativity. Many considered Hawking to have been the successor to Einstein in terms of sheer genius. That's why people took note at some of the comments Hawking made in November 2017.[343]

Hawking said, among other things, that the emergence of artificial intelligence (AI) could be the "worst event in the history of our civilization," unless society finds a way to control its development.

The physicist did say that the technology could help eradicate poverty and disease, but admitted its future is uncertain.

Specifically, Hawking stated that "[s]uccess in creating effective AI, could be the biggest event in the history of our civilization. Or the worst. We just don't know. So we cannot know if we will be infinitely helped by AI, or ignored by it and side-lined, or conceivably destroyed by it," Hawking said during the speech.

Hawking also noted that "[u]nless we learn how to prepare for, and avoid, the potential risks, AI could be the worst event in the history of our civilization. It brings dangers, like powerful autonomous weapons, or new ways for the few to oppress the many. It could bring great disruption to our economy."[344] Additionally, AI has the potential to replace people with machines unlike any other prior technology.[345]

---

343 *Stephen Hawking predictions: supra* note 152.

344 *Id.*

345 W. Sherman Rogers, *Building Social and Human Capital in the Black Community by Increasing Strategic Relationships, Cooperative Economics, the Black Marriage Rate, and the Level of Educational Attainment and Targeted Occupational Training,* 17 Hastings Race & Poverty L.J. 211, 229–230 (2020).
Available at: https://repository.uchastings.edu/hastings_race_poverty_law_journal/vol17/iss2/3

### e. Other Dire Warnings

A *Washington Post* Editorial noted that "[f]or years, people worried about AI and robots taking over popular jobs such as truck driving. Instead, AI is threatening a lot of 'white-collar' jobs' since it has gotten really good at languages, speech recognition, and even decision-making.

"AI can now predict diabetes, protect against cyberthreats and even write term papers and articles. The bots are getting better, and that's something for humans to (mostly) cheer about." Artificial intelligence (AI) has the ability to improve life dramatically.

However, there is now considerable research suggesting the ability of AI to destroy humanity. Nevertheless, some experts in the industry predict that no meaningful regulation will likely occur because of the money to be made by those with the ability to control the technology. Accordingly, regulation may only be forthcoming after a series of well-documented catastrophes occur. But, then, it may be too late.

Experts have said that some AI programs are currently sentient—i.e., AI currently can perceive and feel things. This includes emergent properties to be creative, to reason, and to plan; and the capability of thinking for themselves as humans. Accordingly, leading experts now say that there is every reason to believe that AI will be able to take control of itself. Geoffrey Hinton, known as the godfather of AI, says that smarter-than-human AI could be here in 5 to 20 years, compared with earlier estimates of 30 to 100 years.

Current risks include, among others, unleashing bots trained on racist and sexist information gathered from the web and distributing it in a manner that reinforces those ideas; making up false information and passing it off as factual; increasing social inequities; making the Internet even more skewed away from languages and cultures of most of humanity (because the majority of AI data training is done in English, North America, or Europe); disrupting high paying professions like law and medicine; creating copyright chaos; creating gaping holes in digital privacy and surveillance;

and allowing governments to deploy deadly weapons that can kill without human control.[346]

### 18. Whether the GameStop Stock Trading Mania in "Meme" Stocks was the Inevitable Result of Decades of Lax Regulation?

#### a. Meme Stocks and Reddit's WallStreetBets Online Message Board

Commentators refer to the stocks of companies such as GameStop, Bed, Bath & Beyond, and AMC Entertainment and Blackberry as "meme" stocks.[347]A meme stock is a stock that has seen an increase in trading volume and price because of hype on social media and online forums like Reddit. However, the stock's increase in trading value and price is unconnected to how well the company is performing. Indeed, in many instances, the companies are struggling and may be headed toward bankruptcy.[348]

There appear to be no laws in place to protect investors from market price manipulation of meme stocks on the part of individual retail investors using online forums, such as the Reddit message board, or professional short sellers.

---

346 *22 Good Things That Happened in 2022*, WASH. POST, Editorial, December 25, 2022, at A18 ( Number 20 titled: AI is Having a Moment), Opinion|22 good things that happened in 2022
*Washington Post* https://www.washingtonpost.com › 2022/12/19 › goo... ; Gerrit de Vynck, *AI's Potential for Mayhem is Polarizing Silicon Valley*, WASH. POST, (May 22, 2023), A1.
347 Hamza Shaban, *Bed Bath & Beyond Enjoyed a "Meme Stock" Resurgence: Shares Soar on Digital Plans, Partnership With Kroger, Buybacks News*, Wash Post, November 4, 2021, at A 26., Bed Bath & Beyond enjoys meme stock resurgence *Washington Post* https://www.washingtonpost.com › 2021/11/03 › bed-...
348 Erin Gobler, *What is a Meme Stock?*-The Balance, www.thebalance.com/what-is-a-meme-stock-5118074; Charles Rotblut, *Reddit, Robinhood, and Lessons From the Meme Craze, an Interview With Spencer Jakab*, Author of THE REVOLUTION THAT WASN'T, GAMESTOP, REDDIT AND THE FLEECING OF SMALL INVESTORS AAII Journal, April 2022, at 7, Reddit, Robinhood and Lessons From the Meme Stock Craze American Association of Individual Investors https://www.aaii.com › journal › article › 16673-reddi..

The freedom inherent in American capitalism seems unwilling to create a new rule that would cover their behavior. In the meantime, unsophisticated investors will have to learn the hard way when their investments in these companies inevitably tank.

"Thanks to traders talking it up on social media, the stock of GameStop Corp., the unprofitable mall retailer of video games, climbed as much as 1,745% from the start of the year [in 2021]. The AMC movie theater chain peaked at a gain of 839%; Blackberry and Nokia, which once made very popular phones people strapped to their belts, spiked 279% and 68% respectively; and Koss (headphone maker) and Build-a-Bear Workshop (chain of stores . . .), Tootsie Roll Industries . . . all shot up."

But the failure of Bed, Bath & Beyond in 2023 (and other meme stocks likely to suffer the same fate) provides a cautionary tale of what probably lies ahead for many unsophisticated retail investors engaged in social media hype on social media platforms such as WallStreetBets.[349]

The frequently profane Reddit message board WallStreetBets (WSB), where posters talk about stocks and often band together to try to move prices is the cause of all the frenzy. WallStreetBets "has its own insider language: 'stonks' for stocks and 'tendies' for gains, because chicken tenders are a reward for being good (and because it's funny)."

"Lots of WSB posters don't buy stocks directly but instead use options, which allow them to take big positions for a relatively small amount of money, a form of leverage that amplifies potential gains as well as risks. They also like to go after the so-called shorts, investors who bet against stocks because they believe that a company's stock will decline in market value because of financial problems at the company."

Short sellers borrow shares of meme stocks from their brokers and sell them at today's price with the hope that they can purchase them at a much

---

349 Pat Regnier, *Well, That Was Weird: Tendies, GameStop, Silver, SPACS. What. The. Hell.: A Sane Person's Guide to a Bonkers Stonks Market*, Bloomberg Business Week, February 8, 2021, at 44, Well, That Was Weird Magzter https://www.magzter.com › Bloomberg-Businessweek.

lower price before returning the borrowed shares to the lender. The difference between the higher sales price and the lower purchase price is how the shorts make money.[350] However, "the WSB traders' strategy was that if they could push up the price of the highly shorted stock, the WSB crowd could 'squeeze' the shorts into protecting themselves by buying the stock themselves, triggering a (temporary) upward spiral."[351] There are currently no laws that effectively address the dangers in engaging in either of these activities.

As the WSB group of retail investors pushed the stock higher, the professional traders at the hedge funds collectively faced billions of dollars in losses as the market moved against them.[352] Confronted with these market conditions, various online trading platforms that primarily served retail investors, notably Robinhood, began to suspend purchases of GameStock shares along with other meme stocks that retail investors discussed on WSB. In light of these events, some members of Congress denounced Robinhood's halt in trading as contrary to free market principles. Thereafter, the U.S. House Committee on Financial Services announced hearings to examine predatory conduct by hedge funds.[353]

Specifically, some members of Congress condemned the activity of hedge funds and other large investment firms that were shorting meme stocks as the equivalent of treating the stock market like a personal casino.[354] Moreover, WSB Twitter posts accused hedge funds and large investment firms of colluding to push down prices by publishing scripted research and sharing short sale strategies to manipulate market prices downward and guarantee winning bets.[355]

---

350 We shall briefly discuss the mechanics of short selling after outlining the general transactions involved in the GameStop trading mania.

351 Pat Regnier, *supra* note 349.

352 Haley Van Broekahoven, *SEC Proposes New Rules to Protect Retail Investors From Wall Street Sellers,* http://www.theracetothebottom.org>rttb>sec-propo...

353 The Law of r/WallStreetBets https://www.butzel.com › alert-The-Law-of-r-WallStre...

354 *Id.*

355 Haley Van Broekahoven, *supra* note 352.

On the other hand, some have questioned whether the purchases of meme stocks by retail investors communicating on WSB amounted to market manipulation for the purposes of causing the market price of meme stocks to rise.[356]

These retail investors purchased stocks on credit through trading apps such as Robinhood, through what is known as margin accounts. Purchasing stock in margin accounts only required that the retail investors put up 50 percent of the purchase price of the meme stocks. Therefore, they were partially using Robinhood's money to make their purchases.[357]

However, brokers like Robinhood have their own brokers known as clearinghouses. Clearinghouses must be very vigilant because broker-dealer firms are mutualized. This means if one broker-dealer goes bust, every other broker must chip in to make up for the loss. Therefore, clearinghouses must make sure that broker-dealers such as Robinhood are good for the money that Robinhood's customers owed to Robinhood.

In this case, the clearinghouse calculated that Robinhood needed to pony up $3 billion in case GameStop's stock should drop in price and Robinhood's retail customers could not repay Robinhood. Consequently, Robinhood needed to deposit the $3 billion with the clearinghouse. This is why Robinhood suspended purchases on GameStock shares.[358]

Before we go any further, however, let's briefly discuss the mechanics of short selling.

## b. Short Selling Basics

Hedge fund managers and other well-capitalized financial professional stock traders regularly engage in a practice known as short selling. For purposes of illustration, we'll use a hedge fund manager who engages in a short-selling transaction.

Short selling takes place when the hedge fund manager believes that stock of a company will decline in market value. The manager borrows shares from

---

356 The Law of r/WallStreetBets, *supra* note 353.
357 Charles Rotblut, *supra* note 348, at 9–10.
358 *Id.*

its broker or bank and sells the shares at today's price with the hope of being able to purchase the stock at a lower price prior to returning the borrowed stock to its broker or bank.

Whenever the manager's opening transaction consists of the manager's sale of a company's stock that the investor has borrowed, market professionals refer to this as taking a "short position" in the target company's stock.[359]

For example, a professional stock market trader for a hedge fund may believe that GameStop has an outdated business model and may be out of business in a few years. However, the share price of GameStop has not yet begun to decline but the hedge fund manager believes that it will. This creates a situation in which the hedge fund manager will sell GameStop's shares short.

Here are the steps in the transaction:

- The hedge fund manager borrows 20,000 shares of GameStop from its broker. Because the manager borrowed the 20,000 shares from its broker, the manager must return the 20,000 shares to the broker at some point.

- The hedge fund manager sells the GameStop shares that it borrowed from its broker for $101.00/share. Therefore, the hedge fund has $2,020,000 ($2 million, 20 thousand) in the hedge fund's account.

- The 20,000 GameStop shares the hedge fund manager sold for $101.00 per share are now selling for $1.00 per share.

- Now, the hedge fund manager goes back to the market and purchases 20,000 shares of GameStop for $1.00 per share. This allows the hedge fund manager to repurchase 20,000 shares of GameStop that the hedge fund manager sold for $2,020,000 for only $20,000.

---

359 VIRGINIA MORRIS, *supra* note 295, at 64–65.

- ◆ The hedge fund can now return the 20,000 shares it borrowed from its broker and keep the difference of $2,000,000. The $2,000,000 profit represents the difference between the hedge fund's higher sales price and the fund's lower purchase price. Therefore, as you can see, an investor can make money if the company believes that a company's stock is declining in value.[360]

## c. Robinhood Markets Trading Platform

Robinhood Markets, the zero-commission trading platform, has been the gateway for many young investors to get into the game by allowing investors to purchase fractions of a stock. "Robinhood makes options trading on smartphones easy and nudges users into setting up margin accounts so they can speculate on stock with borrowed money."[361]

## d. Did the Hedge Funds and the Retail Investors Engage in Unlawful Market Manipulation?

"Market manipulation occurs when the price of a security is not determined by the natural interplay of supply and demand and violates the antifraud provisions of the federal securities acts." It takes place when market participants inject "inaccurate information into the market or by creating a false impression of market activity through deceptive trading activities."[362]

It is questionable whether hedge funds or WSB retail investors engaged in market manipulation. This is because market manipulation requires fraud or deception. It is for this reason that some commentators believe that it

---

360 *Id.*

361 Prasanna Mohanty, *Rebooting Economy I: Why Stock Market is Booming When Covid-19-Hit Economy Sinks*, July 2, 2020, www. businesstoday.com, Rebooting Economy I: Why stock market is booming when ...Business Today https://www.businesstoday.in › . . . › Economy Politics; Joseph Heath, *Fractional Investors Stoke Stampede: Ability to Buy Shares of Pricey Names is Hit With Millennials*, WASH. POST, July 12, 2020, at G1.

362 CHERYL NICHOLS, BROKER-DEALER REGULATION 754–770 (2017), and producing excerpts from the case of Sharette v. Suisse Intern, 127 F. Supp. 3d 60 (S.D.N.Y. 2015).

would be difficult to prove a case of manipulation against any of the parties. Accordingly, there appears to be no legal recourse against any of the parties for either harm caused to other investors or harm caused to the integrity of the market.[363]

Economist John Maynard Keynes noted that in many respects the stock market is just a rich person's casino.[364] But, now, the ability of small investors to purchase small fractions of a share of a stock through broker-dealer platforms such as Robinhood, So-Fi, Interactive Brokers, Charles Schwab's Stock Slices (and others) at no commission have ramped up purchases.[365]

A lot of small investors who purchase GameStop and other meme stocks will likely be badly hurt as the fundamental financial weakness of the meme companies cause their prices to decline as some of them head for possible bankruptcy. The 2023 demise of Bed, Bath & Beyond serves as an excellent example of what these investors face.

However, as a general proposition, people do not like others to dictate to them what they can and cannot do—especially when it is the government that is mandating the prohibition. Instead, people generally want to have the right to make voluntary choices without government interference. However, the lack of rules often leads to chaos.

Economist Robert P. Murphy does not believe that any of these potential harms to investors or to the integrity of the market are grounds for government regulation. In his view, speculators, hedgers, short sellers, corporate raiders, and other market players benefit society and that any government effort to thwart their activities will only make society poorer.[366] Murphy believes that "when government intervenes in the market, it not only tramples on freedom, and individual rights, but it also often hurts the very people it presumes to help." Accordingly, in this scenario at least, it is unlikely that the government will do anything to protect investors or the integrity of the markets from these

363  The Law of r/WallStreetBets, *supra* note 353.
364  PAUL KRUGMAN, *supra* note 283, at 134.
365  Prasanna Mohanty, *supra* note 361; Joseph Heath, *supra* note 361.
366  ROGERS, *supra* note 11, at 237.

trading tactics. However, on occasion, the SEC has *temporarily* banned short selling to avert a financial crisis.[367]

### 19. Whether the Hard Freeze in Texas in 2021 Exposed the Dangers of Texas' Deregulated and Independent Electric Power Grid?

Texas has long prided itself on its laissez-faire wholesale energy markets that dates back to the 1990s. The Texas grid enjoys little government oversight from the federal government or the State of Texas. And, compared to other states, the Texas power grid "has almost no regulatory safeguards to ensure sufficient energy is available when demand spikes.[368]

As one commentator noted:

Since at least the Reagan era, the GOP has worshiped at the altar of deregulation. Politicians promulgated the myth that all regulation is anti-growth and, therefore, any regulatory rollback is inherently pro-growth. In particular, they touted the Texas energy market as a sort of paragon of their deregulatory fantasy, an invisible-hand success story that should be expanded nationwide. . . .[369]

Indeed, Texas politicians are so averse "to the idea of government intervention that most of the state is not connected to interstate grids. This exempts the Texas energy system from the purview of a federal regulatory commission. It also means that the state cannot borrow energy from neighbors if its grid

---

367 *Id.* at 216. During the Great Recession of 2008, the SEC *temporarily banned* investors from short selling the stock of 799 financial companies to prevent the stock of these companies from becoming worthless. *Id.* at 434–436. However, the free market casino in stock trading is still very much alive.

368 Catherine Rampell, *Texas's Freeze Exposed the Danger of Deregulation*, WASH. POST, February 23, 2022, at A 25, Opinion | Republicans fearmonger about regulation, but ...*Washington Post*
https://www.washingtonpost.com › 2021/02/22.

369 *Id.*

fails."[370] As a result, the U.S. has divided the power grid into three sections: the first serves the east, the second serves the west, and the third "is reserved for state of Texas. Power generated by Texans, for Texans."[371]

Moreover, the state refused to even require energy producers to weatherize or maintain reserve margins. The argument was that the free market system of supply and demand would "ensure there were no energy shortages or service disruptions." They reasoned that when demand for energy is high, prices would rise. As a result, the politicians assumed that this would incentivize producers to switch on facilities that would otherwise be offline. And that these moneymaking prospects would "induce companies to invest in the maintenance and weatherization that would *enable* generators to fire up whenever necessary, including during extreme temperatures. Otherwise, they'd miss out on huge windfalls."[372]

Deregulation kept energy prices low and made price competition more cutthroat. And, "[w]ith the likelihood of severe winter cold seemingly remote, energy companies had little incentive to make the (costly) capital investments necessary to weatherize." As a result, the Texas deregulated grid system failed to incentivize producers to invest in the necessary weatherization and maintenance of their equipment as free market theory predicted. Instead, it "led to a race to the bottom."[373]

The February 2021 Texas freeze led to foreseeable consequences based on past experiences in 1989 and 2011. In 2021, those consequences included (1) "widespread, day's long power and heat outages"; (2) "deaths from hypothermia and carbon monoxide poisoning"; (3) "shortages of potable water"; and (4) "surprise energy bills, some above $10,000, for those lucky enough to have even occasionally had power." Significantly, the Texas officials "mostly

---

370 *Id.*
371 Jennifer Nelson, *How the Texas Power Grid Works and Why it Failed,* https://www .investopedia.com/texas-power-grid-5207850.
372 Rampell, *Texas's Freeze . . . , supra* note 368.
373 *Id.*

ignored" federal "recommendations" that would call for the state to require Texas producers to winterize their equipment.[374]

Notwithstanding the human suffering caused by the 2021 freeze, "Republican former governor Rick Perry—a past U.S. energy secretary—declared that Texans [were] willing to suffer extended blackouts for the paramount objective of keeping the feds out of their grid."[375]

As millions of Texans went days without heat, light or water, as store shelves were emptied, as deaths blamed on the cold began to add up, Texas' frenzied and deregulated electricity market opened the door for some companies to reap windfalls that some estimated to mount into the billions of dollars. But other companies were facing stupendous losses. Aneesh Prabhu, an analyst with S&P Global, stated that the situation in Texas amounted to the classic definition of market failure.[376]

Market failure takes place when a voluntary market-based exchange is exceedingly costly or practically impossible to consummate.[377] However, there are some in the neoliberal camp who are unwilling to concede that markets ever fail in view of their contempt for government control and regulation over the free choices of persons and entities.[378]

---

374 *Id.*

375 *Id.*

376 Will Englund, Neena Satija, *Some Companies Get Huge Payday From Texas Freeze: Deregulation of Energy Economy Was Sold as a Win for Consumers,* WASH. POST, February 28, 2021, at A6, As Texans went without heat, light or water, some ...https://www.washingtonpost.com › 2021/02/27 › texas.

377 ROGERS, *supra* note 11, at 59.

378 *Id.*

## C. A Brief Analysis of the Deregulatory Efforts of Donald Trump

### *1. Trump's Attempt to Rollback Civil and Human Rights Regulations in 395 Instances*

The Leadership Conference on Civil and Human Rights compiled a list containing 395 initiatives designed to rollback civil and human rights.[379] The Leadership Conference's opening paragraph noted:

> Since Trump took office in January 2017, his administration has worked aggressively to turn back the clock on our nation's civil and human rights progress.

> The Trump Administration's February 10, 2020 budget proposal for fiscal year 2021 provides some insight on where its values lied. Among other things, the proposal included $1 trillion in cuts to Medicaid and the Affordable Care Act over 10 years, cut the Supplemental Nutrition Assistance Program (SNAP, commonly called the food stamp program) by over $182 billion over 10 years, cut assistance to some people with disabilities under the Social Security Disability Insurance and Supplemental Security Income programs, and reduced the Temporary Assistance for Needy Families (TANF) program by $21 billion over 10 years among other drastic cuts.

This is consistent with the Freedom Caucus' view that government spending on social programs distorts the innovation and free enterprise in our American capitalist economic system and that collective action to solve human social problems is primarily coercive in nature.[380]

The voters did not reelect Trump in 2020. Therefore, the Leadership Conference's analysis covers the Trump administration's rollback of civil and human rights rules and regulations from January 27, 2017 to January 18, 2021.

---

379  https://civilrights.org/trump-rollbacks.

380  *Id.* See also ROGERS, *supra* note 11, at 8; ANKER, *supra* note 1, at 20–21, 27.

Here are few examples.[381]

- **February 27, 2017**—The Department of Justice abandoned the federal government's longstanding position that a Texas voter ID law under legal challenge was intentionally racially discriminatory.

- **March 6, 2017**—A week after Trump called on lawmakers to repeal the Affordable Care Act, House Republicans released a proposal to replace the ACA with a law that would end Medicaid as we know it and defund Planned Parenthood.

- **June 8, 2017**—The Department of Education's Office for Civil Rights (OCR) sent a memo to OCR staff discouraging systemic investigations in favor of individual investigations of discrimination.

- **July 26, 2017**—The FCC rescinded its 2014 Joint Sales Agreement (JSA) guidance which had led to the only increase in television diversity in recent years.

- **September 5, 2017**—Attorney General Jeff Sessions announced that the administration was rescinding the Deferred Action for Childhood Arrivals (DACA) program.

- **November 16, 2017**—The Federal Communications voted to gut Lifeline, the program dedicated to bringing phone and internet service within reach for people of color, low-income people, seniors, veterans, and people with disabilities.

- **January 11, 2018**—The Trump administration released new guidelines that allow states to seek waivers to require Medicaid recipients to work.

---

381 https://civilrights.org/trump-rollbacks/ The examples are, for the most part, direct quotes from the Leadership Conference's compilation.

- **January 16, 2018**—The Consumer Financial Protection Bureau, announced it would reconsider the agency's payday lending rule. Thereafter, on **January 18**, the CFPB, abruptly dropped a lawsuit against four online payday lenders who unlawfully made loans of up to 950 percent APR in at least 17 states.

- **March 5, 2018**—The U.S. Department of Education's Office for Civil Rights released a new Case Processing Manual (CPM) that created greater hurdles for people filing complaints and allowed dismissal of civil rights complaints based on the number of times an individual had filed.

- **March 5, 2018**—A Department of Housing and Urban Development Memo announced that Secretary Ben Carson was considering the revision of the agency's mission statement to remove anti-discrimination language and promises of inclusive communities.

- **April 25, 2018**—The Secretary of Housing and Urban Development, Ben Carson, proposed changes to federal subsidies that could triple rent for some households and make it easier to impose work requirements.

- **May 18, 2018**—The Department of Housing and Urban Development announced it would be publishing three separate notices to indefinitely suspend implementation of the 2015 Affirmatively Furthering Fair Housing Rule.

- **July 3, 2018**—Attorney Jeff Sessions and Education Secretary Betsy DeVos rescinded guidance from the Departments of Justice and Education that provides a roadmap to implement voluntary diversity and integration programs in higher education that the Obama administration had drafted to be consistent with existing Supreme Court holdings on the issue.

- **April 17, 2019**—The Department of Housing and Urban Development proposed a rule (eventually published on May 10) seeking to restrict housing assistance for families with mixed-citizenship status. The agency's own analysis showed that the proposal could lead to 55,000 children becoming temporarily homeless.

- **July 23, 2019**—The Trump administration proposed a rule that could cut more than 3 million people from the Supplemental Nutrition Assistance Program (SNAP)—or food stamps—after Congress blocked similar efforts in 2018.

- **July 31, 2019**—*Bloomberg Law* reported that the Department of Housing and Urban Development (HUD) planned to issue a proposed rule to amend the agency's "disparate impact" regulations that provide anti-discrimination protections to people of color, women, and others. HUD officially published the proposal in the Federal Register on August 19, 2019. The Leadership Conference on Civil and Human Rights stated that, if enacted, millions of people in America would be more vulnerable to housing discrimination as they would have fewer tools to challenge it.

- **November 1, 2019**—The Department of Education issued a final regulation permitting religious colleges and universities to ignore nondiscrimination standards set by accrediting agencies.

- **January 7, 2020**—The Department of Housing and Urban Development issued a proposal that would gut the agency's 2015 Affirmatively Furthering Fair Housing rule. The Leadership Conference on Civil and Human Rights stated that HUD's proposal would leave people of color, women, and protected communities already harmed by unfair and unequal housing policies at further disadvantage.

- **May 6, 2020**—The Department of Education released its final rule on Title IX that raised the bar of proof for sexual misconduct, bolstered the rights of those accused, and introduced new protections for those accused of sexual harassment.

- **June 12, 2020**—The Department of Health and Human Services issued its final rule rolling back the non-discrimination protections (Section 1557) of the Affordable Care Act. According to The Leadership Conference on Civil and Human Rights, the rule would promote discrimination in medical care.

- **July 23, 2020**—HUD Secretary Ben Carson terminated the Obama-era Affirmatively Furthering Fair Housing (AFFH) rule, replacing it with a new rule called "Preserving Community and Neighborhood Choice." The Leadership Conference on Civil and Human Rights noted that the purpose of the AFFH rule was to combat segregation in housing policy.

- **August 26, 2020**—The Department of Education issued a "Dear Educator's and Stakeholders Letter" announcing the withdrawal of eight guidance documents, including in its rationale that previous support the Department expressed for diversity was advocating for "policy preferences and positions beyond the requirements of the Constitution and Title VI."

- **September 4, 2020**—The Department of Housing and Urban Development issued a final rule that severely weakened the disparate impact tool under the Fair Housing Act. In the view of The Leadership Conference on Civil and Human Rights, the rule would make millions of people more vulnerable to housing discrimination.

- **September 4, 2020**—Russell Vought, the Director of the Office of Management and Budget, sent a memo to the heads of executive departments and agencies instructing them to end anti-racist trainings that address White privilege and critical race theory, **calling them "divisive, anti-American propaganda."**

- **September 22, 2020**—Trump issued an executive order prohibiting agencies, federal contractors, and grantees from engaging in anti-discrimination workplace diversity trainings the administration deemed "divisive."

- **October 8, 2020**—A Justice Department memo suspended all diversity and inclusion training for the Department's employees and managers in compliance with Trump's recent executive order banning anti-bias training.

- **October 21, 2020**—Trump signed an executive order that could expand his ability to hire and fire tens of thousands of federal employees. The order would require federal agencies to reclassify certain workers which would strip them of job protections. The national president of the American Federation of Government Employees referred to the order as "the most profound undermining of the civil service in our lifetimes."

- **November 2, 2020**—Trump signed an executive order establishing the President's Advisory 1776 Commission to "promote patriotic education." The Leadership Conference on Civil and Human Rights said that some viewed the Commission as a political move aimed at censoring the teaching of American history and as an attack on *The New York Times'* Pulitizer-Prize winning 1619 Project, which details this nation's history beginning when the British brought the first enslaved Africans to America.

- **January 18, 2020**—On this day, which was the Martin Luther King, Jr. birthday holiday, Trump's 1776 Commission issued a report calling for "patriotic education," comparing progressivism to fascism and communism.

## 2. Trump's Efforts to Weaken Environmental Protections Through 74 Deregulatory Actions

The Brookings Institution, as of August 4, 2020, had counted 74 actions by the Trump administration to weaken environmental protection.[382] Government regulation is not intrinsically inefficient. However, regulations imposed on businesses have occasionally created inefficiencies in the American economy. The Trump administration's activities are consistent with the view that unregulated market forces should determine economic and safety outcomes, not the government.

The Brookings Institution noted that the Trump administration had been particularly focused on rolling back prior actions designed to deal with climate change. Trump promised to withdraw the United States from the Paris Agreement—an agreement among 195 nations to cut their greenhouse gas emissions (GHG). Under the Trump administration, the United States stood alone among major emitters of GHG to repudiate the Paris Agreement.[383]

In 2007, the U.S. Supreme Court found that greenhouse gases were within the Clean Air Act's definition of an air pollutant.[384] The Obama administration used the Clean Air Act to establish the Clean Power Plan. The Clean Power Plan was the foundation for the Obama administration's strategy to reduce GHG admissions. It sought to reduce carbon dioxide ($CO_2$) emissions from

---

382 What is the Trump Administration's Track Record on the Environment? https://www .brookings.edu/.../what-is-the-trump-administrations-track-record-on-the-envoronment.
383 *Id.*
384 Massachusetts v. EPA, 497 (2007).

the power sector and had the effect of prohibiting new coal plants without carbon capture and storage.

The Trump administration replaced the Clean Power Plan with weaker regulations and sought to eliminate other regulations that limit GHG emissions until the end of its term. For example, the Trump administration changed a prior rule that required that fuel economy must improve by 5 percent per year between 2021–2026 to 1.5 percent.[385]

The Trump administration's other regulatory rollbacks were designed to boost fossil fuel production and use. For example, the Trump administration rolled back regulations on airborne emissions of mercury, reduced regulations governing the disposal and storage of coal ash to fulfill Trump's campaign promise to revive the U.S. coal industry. However, coal used in power generation in 2019 was down 22 percent from 2016 due to significant competition from inexpensive natural gas, not regulation. Another example of the Trump administration's goals to boost fossil fuel production and use was Trump's attempts to lift bans on oil and gas exploration on public lands.[386]

The Trump administration's deregulatory actions also sought to rollback protections affecting the nation's core environmental laws that ensure clean air, clean water, and that safeguard sensitive lands. Those actions include: the refusal to strengthen the National Ambient Air Quality Standards (NAAQS) for fine particulate matter and ozone; changes in the composition of advisory committees to include more industry and anti-regulatory members; placing limits on the scientific research that committees could consider; and keeping the pesticide chlorpyrifos on the market despite evidence of its risks.[387]

With respect to decisions of the Trump administration to limit protection of sensitive lands are the following: cutting in half the time for the government to study the environmental impact of a project; limiting the role of climate change in environmental assessments; excluding some projects

---

385 What is the Trump Administration's Track Record on the Environment?, *supra* note 382.

386 *Id.*

387 *Id.*

from the environmental assessment requirement; and limiting water bodies subject to the Clean Water Act.[388] These actions are consistent with the view that when the government intervenes in the market, it tramples on freedom and individual rights and impinges on the free market's ability to achieve maximum efficiency. And often, government regulation hurts the very people it presumes to help.

However, while government regulation is not intrinsically inefficient, it has occasionally created inefficiencies in the economy. However, the lack of rules often leads to chaos.

### 3. Trump's Attempts to Repeal the Patient Protection and Affordable Care Act (Obamacare)

The Trump administration, with few exceptions, took the neoliberal position that government regulatory programs, *including social and welfare programs*, impinge on the free market's ability to achieve maximum efficiency. Accordingly, in the Trump-administration's view, unregulated market forces should determine economic outcomes—not the government. This requires that government not regulate any activity that encroaches on the ability of persons to enter into voluntary exchanges that are mutually acceptable to the parties to the bargain.

Accordingly, Republicans in Congress—guided principally by neoliberal principles—repeatedly sought to repeal the Affordable Care Act. In 2012, the U.S. Supreme Court issued its first ruling upholding the Affordable Care Act. In *National Federation of Independent Business v. Sebelius,*[389] the Court held that Congress had the power under the Constitution's Taxing and Spending Powers to impose the individual mandate—a penalty for not buying health insurance—as a way to fund the Act. However, the majority said the expansion of Medicaid could not take place nationwide as Congress intended. Instead,

---

388 *Id.*
389 567 U.S. 519 (2012).

the Court held that the states must make that decision on a state-by-state basis. This was a partial victory for Republicans.[390]

In 2015, the Court, in *King v. Burwell*,[391] upheld a key portion of the law in a case that had challenged the federal subsidies the ACA provides most people who buy health plans through the insurance marketplaces. The Affordable Care Act states that individuals are eligible for tax credits to help pay for plans who were enrolled in a plan through an "Exchange established by a State." However, the Internal Revenue Service granted the tax credits regardless of whether a State created the exchange or the Department of Health and Human Service. The Court found that, when taken in context, the phrase "established by a State" was ambiguous because other parts of the of the Affordable Care Act treated federal and state exchanges as equivalent and assumed that tax credits would be available through either.[392]

President Trump campaigned on the promise of repealing the Affordable Care Act should the electorate vote him in as President in 2016. And he vowed to end the law legislatively. When Trump came to office in 2017, the Republican Party held control of the Executive branch of government and both the House and the Senate. However, his early efforts failed in mid-2017 due to in-party disputes. John McCain cast the deciding vote against repeal because the Republican's promised replacement legislation was not forthcoming.[393]

In 2017, Congress enacted legislation to repeal the individual mandate by reducing it to zero as part of the Tax Cut and Jobs Act of 2017. Thereafter, Texas and other Republican-led states challenged the Affordable Care Act.

---

390 *Id.*

391 576 U.S. 473 (2015).

392 *Id.*

393 Robert Barnes, *Affordable Care Act Survives Third Challenge, as Case for GOP-led States and Endorsed by the Trump Administration is Rejected*, WASH. POST (June 17, 2021), https://www.washingtonpost.com/politics/courts_law/affordable-care-act-survives-third-supreme-court-challenge-as-case-from-trump-administration-and-gop-led-states-is-rejected/2021/06/17/1d800dce-cf6f-11eb-8cd2-4e95230cfac2_story.html; Heather Long, *The Final GOP Tax Bill is Complete. Here's What's In It.*, WASH. POST, (December 15, 2017), The final GOP tax bill, explained—The *Washington Post* https://www.washingtonpost.com › wonk › 2017/12/15.

They argued that once Congress abolished the individual mandate, the Constitutional basis for the legislation—Congress' taxing powers—had been removed. Trump's Department of Justice declined to defend the case in court. Thereafter, California Attorney General Xavier Becerra, who had subsequently become HHS Secretary for President Biden, led a group of blue states to defend the Act in court.[394]

In 2021, the Court held, in the case of *California v. Texas,*[395] that none of the parties had standing to argue whether the 2017 decision by Congress to remove the individual mandate caused or did not cause the Affordable Care Act to be unconstitutional.

### 4. Trump's Goal to Deregulate the Financial and Energy Sectors

#### a. The Financial Sector

President Trump sought to loosen regulations that the Dodd-Frank Act imposed on financial institutions following the 2007–2008 subprime mortgage crisis. President Trump tweeted on November 25, 2017 that the Act had devastated financial institutions and rendered them unable to serve the public. However, during the period in question, banks had generated a record level of profit and bank stocks were in record territory.[396]

The Trump administration and others also asserted that excessive financial regulation since the passage of Dodd-Frank in 2008 had caused banks, and

---

394 *Id. See also* Margo Sanger Katz, *Democrats Ask Supreme Court for Quick Decision on Obamacare,* N.Y. Times (January 3, 2020), Democrats Ask Supreme Court for Quick Decision on …The New York Times https://www.nytimes.com › 2020/01/03 › upshot › demo…
; Nathaniel Weixel, *GOP States Tell Supreme Court to Wait on Reviewing Obamacare Case,* The Hill ( February 3, 2020).
395  593 U.S. ___, 141 S. Ct. 2104 (2021).
396  Matthew Goldstein, Stacy Cowley, *Casting Wall Street as Victim, Trump Leads Deregulatory Charges,* N. Y. Times.com (November 27, 2017), Casting Wall Street as Victim, Trump Leads Deregulatory …The New York Times https://www.nytimes.com › 2017/11/27 › business › fina.

especially smaller banks, to decline in numbers.[397] However, the FDIC noted that consolidation in the U.S. banking industry had been a multi-decade trend beginning in 1984.[398]

The Dodd-Frank Act, among other things, established the Consumer Protection Regulatory Agency. Trump installed budget director Mick Mulvaney to head the agency despite Mulvaney's staunch opposition to the Agency's past history of issuing broad regulations.

On May 22, 2018, The House and Senate approved a bill rolling back various provisions of the Dodd-Frank Act. And the Fed, in 2019, further loosened regulations. Among the rollbacks were requirements that midsize banks with $50 billion to $250 billion in assets face annual stress tests designed to maintain the financial soundness of banks.

However, after the collapse of Silicon Valley Bank, Signature Bank, and First Republic Bank in March 2023, many have criticized these regulatory rollbacks as being a contributing factor in the failure of these banks. However, conservative politicians put the blame on "woke capitalism." Specifically, they argued that these banks' diversity, equity, and inclusion policies diverted them from focusing on their core missions.[399]

On May 24, Trump signed the Economic Growth, Regulatory Relief and Consumer Protection Act. The law rolled back more expansive Home Mortgage Disclosure data requirements for banks that generate fewer than 500 loans or lines of credit each year. The effect of this provision was

---

397 Becky Yerak, *Is Marco Rubio Right About 40% of Banks Wiped Out by Dodd-Frank?* Is Marco Rubio right about 40% of banks wiped out by ...Chicago Tribune https://www.chicagotribune.com › business › ct-rubio-do..

398 https://www.fdic.gov/regulations/resources/cbi/report/cbi-full.pdf.

399 Congress Approves First Big Dodd-Frank Rollback https://www.nytimes.com › 2018/05/22 › business › cong... ; Pat Regnier and Paula Dwyer, *The Sudden Unmaking of Silicon Valley Bank*, Bloomberg Businessweek, March 20, 2023, at 29; Rachel Siegel, *Reports Shred Banking Controls: Fed Seeks Tighter Reigns After Crisis*, WASH POST, April 29, 2023, at A1; Editorial, *Bank Failures Should Not be Routine*, WASH POST, May 2, 2023; Julian Mark, *Conservative Politicians Put Blame for SVB's Collapse on 'Woke Capitalism,"* WASH POST, March 15, 2023, at A17.

to exempt 85 percent of banks and credit unions from these disclosure requirements.[400]

## b. The Energy Sector

The Trump administration moved broadly to relax Obama-era rules put in place to regulate methane and other greenhouse gas emissions, offshore drilling safety, fuel economy and wetlands rules that impact oil, gas, and coal industries.[401]

The rollbacks came amid surging oil and gas production that put the United States output ahead of historical leaders' Saudi Arabia and Russia. The U.S. Energy Information Administration reported that in May 2017, the United States pumped a record 12.4 million barrels per day of crude.

A priority of the Trump administration was to reduce the regulatory burden on oil and gas companies to drive U.S. energy production and exports. However, environmentalists instituted litigation to block the administration's efforts.[402]

Below is a list of changes to federal oil and gas regulations that the Trump administration implemented or proposed.

## (1) Easing Methane Limits

In August 2017, the administration proposed to roll back limits on methane emissions at oil and gas operations that the Obama administration had implemented.[403]

The proposal sought to repeal Obama administration regulations put in place in 2016 that limit methane emissions from new oil and gas drilling,

---

400 https://civilrights.org/trump-rollbacks.

401 Liz, Hampton, Factbox: U.S. oil and gas regulatory rollbacks under Trump https://www.reuters.com › article › factbox-u-s-oil-and-...

402 *Id.*

403 *Id.*

transport, and storage operations. Natural gas is composed mostly of methane, one of the main pollutants scientists link to climate change.

## (2) Offshore Drilling

In May 2017, the Trump administration unveiled its final plan to roll back offshore drilling safety measures that the Obama administration had enacted following the fatal 2010 Deepwater Horizon oil spill. The Trump administration anticipated that the changes would save oil and gas companies $1 billion over ten years.

The Obama administration's well-control and blowout preventer rule issued in 2016 had required real-time monitoring of operations and certification by third parties of emergency devices. The Sierra Club and other groups sued to reverse the Trump administration's decision, arguing the U.S. had failed to consider potential damage to offshore safety and the environment.[404]

## (3) Power Plant Rules

In June, the Trump administration finalized a carbon emissions rule for U.S. power plants to help the ailing coal industry and replaced an Obama-era rule targeted at fighting climate change.

The Trump administration's Affordable Clean Energy (ACE) rule would give states three years to devise their own plans to cut emissions, primarily by encouraging coal-fired power plants to improve their efficiency.[405]

## (4) Expansion of Offshore Drilling

In 2017, the Trump administration ordered a reversal of an Obama-era ban on oil and gas drilling in the Arctic and Atlantic oceans. In 2018, it outlined a proposal to open up the Atlantic, Pacific and new parts of the Arctic oceans to offshore drilling.

---

404 *Id.*
405 *Id.*

Since the Trump administration announced its plan, six states passed legislation or amendments to restrict offshore drilling. However, a court ruling to block drilling in the Atlantic and Arctic sidelined the plan.

### (5) Paris Accord Withdrawal

Trump announced in 2017 that he would withdraw the U.S. from the Paris Agreement. The Paris Accord seeks to limit global warming to less than 2 degrees Celsius (3.6 degrees Fahrenheit). Achieving that goal would cut as much as 40 percent off oil demand by the early 2040s, impacting the industry, according to investment fund Legal and General Investment Management.

In a symbolic move, the U.S. House of Representatives in May approved a bill calling on the president to develop a plan to meet the agreement's goals. However, the U.S. Senate refused to consider it.[406]

### (6) Pipeline Permitting

In 2019, Trump issued executive orders to limit the ability of states to block interstate energy projects, including pipelines, under a provision of the U.S. Clean Water Act. Trump's orders called for a review of rules requiring state certifications for federally approved interstate pipelines and project.[407]

## 5. Trump's Aim to Preside Over the Response to the Covid-19 Pandemic through a Liberty-Based, Decentralized Approach

The U.S.'s disjointed response to Covid-19 staggered the world, resulting in by far the highest case and death count globally. The die was cast by two fundamental policy decisions taken by the Trump administration.[408] Those

---

406 *Id.*

407 *Id.*

408 Drew Altman, *Understanding the US Failure on Coronavirus*, https://doi .org/10.1136/bmj.m3417 (Published 14 September 2020).

decisions were the use of the federal government in a back-up role to the states and the politicization of the pandemic response.

### a. The Federal Government as Back-up

After first casting himself as a wartime president, in April 2020, President Trump made a fundamental policy shift that shaped the U.S. response to the pandemic. Trump announced that the states would have primary responsibility for containing the virus, with the federal government in a "back-up" role.[409]

A state role in public health is traditional in the U.S., and any national plan would allow for customization to reflect regional and state circumstances. However, delegating primary responsibility to states in a crisis was unprecedented.

Trump's decision was consistent with conservative principles to let state and local governments customize solutions to local circumstances. However, the decision may have been an effort to offload political accountability for a growing pandemic with the presidential election looming.[410]

The ramifications of the Trump administration's decision was disastrous. In the absence of a centralized federal response, the fragmentation between states, counties, and cities in filling the vacuum left by the federal government's failure to lead resulted in extreme variation in the U.S. response to Covid-19 by and within the states. As a result, some states opened up their economies earlier than others. In general, the states that opened up their economies earlier suffered larger outbreaks.[411]

This led directly to the second fateful policy decision shaping the U.S. response. The Trump administration, apparently for political reasons, decided to push to open up the economy before the virus was contained. This had the result of fracturing the country along partisan lines.

---

409 *Id.*

410 *Id.*

411 *Id.*

### b. A Starkly Partisan Pandemic Response

President Trump initially pushed for opening the economy as early as Easter of 2020. However, the Trump administration had to move that timetable back in the face of the reality that Covid-19 infections and deaths had continued to surge.

Trump's response caused the American people to split along partisan lines in their response to Covid-19, as if the country had both red and blue pandemics. When that happened, the public's willingness to prevent the spread of the virus substantially collapsed across red America.

The partisan divide could be seen on almost every dimension of the epidemic. Democrats were about twice as likely as Republicans to say the worst was yet to come on the pandemic and a wide gulf opened between Democrats and Republicans on the opening of schools.

The decentralized structure of the U.S. response could have worked more effectively had the role of the federal government as "back-up" been buttressed by a national plan overlaying the states' responses to the crisis. However, the Trump administration's response was entirely consistent with the historical beginnings of the U.S.: specifically, the efforts on the part of the southern states and others to limit the reach of the federal government to preserve the liberty rights of slave owners and other entrepreneurs to be free to engage in business without interference from a controlling federal government.[412]

In the United States, the government has only enacted major economic and social welfare legislation as a matter of last resort. This is due, in part, to Americans' traditional suspicion of centralized power and authority. Thus, government regulation in the U.S. tends to be reactive and rarely proactive.

---

412 ROGERS, *supra* note 11, at 54–57 (libertarianism); 155–157 (characteristics of a capitalistic economic system); 216 (when government intervenes in the market, it tramples on freedom and individual rights); 261 (the U.S. did not have a central bank until 1913 because of Americans "traditional suspicion of centralized power and authority"); 311, 314 (until the 1930s, the U.S. had a very small government); 350 (the founders designed the first federal debt deal to keep the states in control of the right to maintain slavery).

# PART IV

# THE IDEAL APPROACH TO GOVERNMENT REGULATION AND SOCIAL WELFARE LEGISLATION

A *system of regulated capitalism operating* under a government welfare economic approach is the best way to ensure a better future for all people. No nation in the 21ˢᵗ century has yet to adopt the libertarian utopian state of a bare-bones, minimalist government, and it is unlikely that any nation will.[413]

This book takes the position that a government's decision to regulate in the areas of social justice and government welfare laws be based on John Rawls' "a theory of justice." As one commentator noted, "[c]entral to the Rawlsian model is the belief that people are risk-averse." Indeed, "[t]hey are so risk-averse that they adopt a decision-making rule called 'maximin.' Under a maximin rule, [people] assume they will ultimately be among the worst off in society and then choose the governing principles that would maximize the welfare of the worst off."[414]

Under Rawls' view, "each individual would have a right to the most extensive basic liberty compatible with a similar liberty for others." Additionally, "social and economic inequalities would be arranged so that they are reasonably

---

413 *Id.* at 54.
414 HARRISON, *supra* note 1, at 439

expected to be to everyone's advantage. This second principle—called the 'difference principle'—would allow for inequalities in income and wealth, but those who become better off could only do so if those at the bottom of the distribution are also made better off."[415]

---

415 *Id.* at 438.

# PART V

# CONCLUSION

This book has attempted to demonstrate how people and entities often rely on notions of freedom, liberty, personal sovereignty, government sovereignty, and neoliberalism: (1) as defenses to their conduct regardless of whether it causes harm to others, and (2) as grounds to avoid government regulation and liability for their actions.[416]

Ironically, persons have also used freedom and liberty-based arguments to suppress or even destroy the liberty rights of others throughout the history of the United States. They also seem willing to put themselves in harm's way in the name of freedom. Typically, they base their rationale on individual freedom against government paternalism, personal sovereignty to make final decisions about life and death, and the primacy of individual choice over public needs.

Consequently, many tolerate gun violence, an emerging climate disaster, a dangerous reduction in the social safety net, and a host of preventable injuries all in the name of freedom. Sometimes, they base their positions on the right to be free *from* government regulation. However, on other occasions, they

---

416 ELISABETH R. ANKER, UGLY FREEDOMS 1–16, 89 (2022). The term, "externality," refers to the actions of persons—both individuals and entities—that affect others. A negative externality exists when a person's acts affect others unfavorably and the person causing the harm does not pay the person harmed for the injury caused. A positive externality exists when a person's acts affect others in a favorable manner and the person receiving the benefit does not pay the person providing the benefit. JEFFREY L. HARRISON and JULES THEEUWES, LAW AND ECONOMICS 58–59 (2008). Most government regulation concerns efforts to respond to negative externalities. JEFFREY L. HARRISON, LAW AND ECONOMICS IN A NUTSHELL 328, 335 (5TH Ed. 2011).

justify policies that may even cause them harm on the freedom *to* engage in certain activities.

However, one need not take a normative stance on the ethics of those who use a liberty-based defense to recognize the defense for how it is often used—*as a means to avoid liability for harming others.* Accordingly, those who have used or may use liberty-based defenses to justify acts that harm others should not feel demeaned. Indeed, the U.S. Constitution's protections of freedom and liberty have proved to be "notoriously contested concept[s] as [their] meaning continuously shifts in different historical moments."[417]

A good illustration of the contested nature of what freedom means can be seen in the contrasting views of Florida governor Ron DeSantis and the editorial board of the *Washington Post*. On one hand, Florida governor Ron DeSantis refers to Florida as "a citadel of freedom," "freedom's linchpin," "freedom's vanguard," and "on the front lines of freedom." The editors of the *Washington Post*, however, see DeSantis' policies as a direct attack on freedom in Florida. In the *Post's* view, "Mr. DeSantis is waging frontal assaults on press freedom, reproductive freedom, free enterprise and academic freedom."

The *Post's* editors do not stop there. They also maintain that DeSantis, "in the name of protecting gun rights, has scaled back prudent safety rules" and is "now poised to target undocumented immigrants, including 'dreamers,' with what will be some of the cruelest policies in America."

An even more striking illustration of the contested nature of freedom can be seen in the Southern Poverty Law Center's June 2023 declaration that an organization called **Moms for Liberty** can be correctly labeled as an "extremist group" devoted to spreading "messages of anti-inclusion and hate," "conspiracy theories" and "actions to censor school discussions around race, discrimination, and LGBTQ+ identities."

The protection of the liberty rights of slave owners— and business owners generally—to engage in commercial activities without interference from a controlling federal government has been a prominent theme in American

---

417 ANKER, *supra* note 1, at 2.

history. Consequently, there are frequent clashes between the desire of persons to be free of government regulation and the role of government to pass laws to protect society generally as well as certain vulnerable members of society.

Two recent studies indicate that persons who reside in conservative congressional districts—characterized by leaders who champion *small government, freedom from mask requirements, freedom from federal programs that support social welfare programs, freedom from federal health and welfare initiatives*, and *freedom from regulations involving the environment and gun safety*, while *also seeking to ban abortions*—have significantly higher mortality rates than persons who live in jurisdictions that take the opposite approach.[418] Therefore, it is entirely consistent that the most conservative group in Congress refers to itself as the "Freedom Caucus."[419]

Columnist Fareed Zakaria, in a 2017 *Washington Post* article titled "The Populist Plutocrats March On," explored the reasons why people may support policies that may not be to their advantage. Zakaria observed that the most important revolution in economics in the past generation has been the rise of behavioral scientists, trained in psychology, *who are finding that people systematically make decisions that are against their own "interests."* The research, he noted, indicates that people may actually be motivated far more deeply by issues surrounding religion, race and culture than they are by economics.

In Zakaria's view, these studies "might be the tip of the iceberg in understanding human motivation." The real story, he noted, might be that people see their own interests in a much more emotional and tribal way than scholars understand. Zakaria openly wondered whether, in the eyes of a large group of

---

418 Akilah Johnson, *supra* note 8. In the December 22, 2022 study, The Harvard T. H. Chan School of Public Health. performed a study examined the health and longevity outcomes in each of the 435 congressional districts as well as state legislatures. In the other study, two University of Washington professors published a study in October, 2022, that found that conservative leaning jurisdictions could have avoided the deaths of hundreds of thousands of their citizens if they had implemented policies enacted by liberal jurisdictions in the areas of abortion, the environment, gun safety, criminal justice, health and welfare, and economic and tobacco taxes.

419 ROGERS, *supra* note 11, at 8.

Americans, issues involving religion, race, and culture are the ones for which people will stand up, protest, support politicians and even pay an economic price. Thus, Zakaria pondered whether "for many people, in America and around the world, these are their true interests."

In the United States, the government has only enacted major economic and social welfare legislation as a matter of last resort. This is due, in part, to Americans' traditional suspicion of centralized power and authority. Thus, government regulation in the U.S. tends to be reactive and rarely proactive.

Examples of crises in America that have produced major legislation include the Civil War, the rise of business monopolies in the latter part of the 1800s, the bank panic of 1907 (which eventually led the U.S. to establish the Federal Reserve System), the collapse of the stock markets in 1929, the Great Depression of the 1930s, World War I, World War II, the Civil Rights Movement of the 1950s and 1960s, the collapse of Enron Corporation, the Great Recession of 2008, and the Covid-19 Recession of 2020 (aka the Great Lockdown).

This book has shown that freedom is a "notoriously contested concept." Indeed, freedom has been used to justify "slavery, indigenous dispossession, environmental destruction, sex and gender oppression, and the violent machinations of a 'free' market that enable the powerful few to accumulate vast wealth amid widespread poverty and homelessness."[420] Therefore, it is not surprising that freedom often "ignores the appalling violence that traffics under its name."[421]

It is for these reasons that this book maintains that government should attempt to improve social safety net programs to provide for universal healthcare, housing, daycare, and greater subsidization for food. These goals are not hostile to notions of free market capitalism and freedom of choice.[422] Indeed, even neoliberal theorists have recognized that government intervention is warranted in the provision of public goods and services where it would be

---

420 ANKER, *supra* note 1, at 2 and 4.
421 *Id.* at 14.
422 ROGERS, *supra* note 11, at 121–127.

exceedingly costly and inefficient for the private sector to provide certain goods and services.[423]

In light of the foregoing, it should not be surprising that the research of epidemiologists Richard Wilson and Kate Pickett indicate that countries, like the U.S., that have greater economic inequality, spend less of their national income on social services than peer countries. The findings of Wilson and Pickett also determined that the U.S. and other countries that spend less of their national income on social services had greater rates of teen pregnancy, infant mortality, mental illness, drug use, imprisonment, and homicide than countries where wealth is more evenly distributed.[424]

Therefore, this book takes the position that government does not infringe on the freedom of entities and persons when it enacts targeted, smart, regulation of persons and entities sufficient to assure the health, safety, and general welfare of its people in the least burdensome manner and when it spends a sufficient amount of the nation's revenues to maintain a viable social safety net for its inhabitants.

But not all government regulation is "smart" regulation. It only took 1 year and 45 days for contractors to build the Empire State Building from its March 17, 1930 starting date. However, it took Georgia 14 years to complete a $1 billion infrastructure project largely because of environmental and regulatory hurdles. Regardless of one's political affiliation, it certainly appears that, in some instances, government regulation may be objectively excessive. And, while government regulation isn't intrinsically inefficient, it has occasionally created inefficiencies in the American economy.

Thus, it is quite understandable why some politicians and economists believe that government should eliminate many of the regulations that it imposes on businesses and entrepreneurs. In the view of some, when government intervenes in the market, it not only tramples on freedom and individual rights, but often hurts the very people it presumes to help. They believe, with few exceptions, that government regulatory programs, including

---

423 *Id.* at 30–31, 59–61, 101–102, 214–215.
424 *Id.* at 320.

social and welfare programs, impinge on the free market's ability to achieve maximum efficiency. Accordingly, in their view, unregulated market forces should determine economic outcomes—not the government. This requires that government not regulate any activity that encroaches on the ability of persons to enter into voluntary exchanges that are mutually acceptable to the parties to the bargain.

But the discussion of regulation tends to be much more complex. For example, artificial intelligence (AI) has the ability to dramatically improve life as we know it. However, there is now considerable research suggesting that AI has the ability to destroy humanity. This book has discussed some of these alarming findings. Indeed, we are currently seeing some of the dark sides of AI. Nevertheless, some experts in the industry predict that no meaningful regulation will likely occur because of the money to be made by those with the ability to control the technology. Accordingly, regulation may only be forthcoming after a series of well-documented catastrophes occur. This is typically what must happen before regulation takes place in America. However, by then, it may be too late.

Most government regulation concerns efforts to respond to externalities[425] and the reduction of transaction costs for consumers.[426] These are appropriate responses by government in protecting persons from harmful behavior of others. Accordingly, the thesis of this book is that a system of regulated capitalism operating under a government welfare economic approach to capitalism does not interfere with the freedom of persons or entities and is the best way to ensure a better future for all people.

---

425 ROGERS, *supra* note 11, at 64–68. HARRISON, *supra* note 29, at 328, 335.
426 HARRISON, *supra* note 1, at 328–335. *See also* at 77–103.

# BIBLIOGRAPHY

## Articles and Book Chapter in Multi-authored Books

Allsup, Maeve. "Gig Companies Face California Crackdowns That Uber, Lyft Escape." Gig Companies Face California Crackdowns That Uber, Lyft …bloomberglaw.com https://news.bloomberglaw.com › daily-labor-report

Altman, Drew. "Understanding the US Failure on Coronavirus." https://doi .org/10.1136/bmj.m3417 (Published 14 September 2020).

Anker, Elizabeth. "The Exploitation of 'Freedom'" *N.Y. Times* (February 6, 2022), at 6 of Sunday Review, Opinion | Freedom Is a Bad Defense for Ugly Behavior *The New York Times*
https://www.nytimes.com › 2022/02/04 › opinion › ugly…

Asare, Janice Gassam. "Does TikTok Have A Race Problem?" *Forbes* (Apr. 14, 2020, 12:42 AM), https://www.forbes.com/sites/janicegassam/2020/04/14 /does-tiktok-have-a-race-problem/?sh=7ae3ed1c3260.

Barnes, Robert. "Affordable Care Act Survives Third Challenge, as Case for GOP-led States and Endorsed by the Trump Administration is Rejected." *Washington Post* (June 17,2021), https://www.washingtonpost .com/politics/courts_law/affordable-care-act-survives-third-supreme -court-challenge-as-case-from-trump-administration-and-gop-led- states-is-rejected/2021/06/17/1d800dce-cf6f-11eb-8cd2–4e95230cfac2_ story.html.

Barnes, Robert. "Justices Hold Testy Debate on Free Speech: Designer Who Wants to Refuse Same-Sex Clients Seems to Win Sympathy." *Washington Post* (December 6, 2022), at A1 (mentioning the role of the Alliance

Defending Freedom's representation of the website designer), Wedding websites are the latest gay rights battleground in ...*Washington Post* https://www.washingtonpost.com › 2022/12/04 › colo...

Brady, Patrick G., Schlegel, Julie Saker. "Trump Administration's DOL Rejects Obama-Era Guidance on" ...wagehourblog.comhttps://www.wagehourblog.com › FLSA Coverage.

Brogan, Jacob. "Your Algorithms Cheat Sheet." Slate (Feb. 2, 2016, 10:28 AM), https://slate.com/technology/2016/02/algorithms-101-a-cheat-sheet-to-the-terminology-the-ethical-debates-and-more.html.

de Vynck, Gerrit. "AI's Potential for Mayhem is Polarizing Silicon Valley. *Washington Post*, (May 22, 2023). A1.

Deion, E.J., Jr. "Biden Looks to Challenge Republicans on Freedom." *Washington Post*, (May 1, 2023), A19.

Downs, Anthony. "Residential Rent Controls: An Evaluation." Urban Land Institute (1988), Residential Rent Controls University of California, Irvine https://www.socsci.uci.edu › ~jkbrueck › Downs.

Englund, Will, Satija, Neena. "Some Companies Get Huge Payday From Texas Freeze: Deregulation of Energy Economy Was Sold as a Win for Consumers." *Washington Post* ( February 28, 2021), at A6, As Texans went without heat, light or water, some ...https://www.washingtonpost.com › 2021/02/27 › texas.

Gobler, Erin. "What is a Meme Stock?" The Balance, www.thebalance.com/what-is-a-meme-stock-5118074

Goldstein, Matthew, Cowley, Stacy. "Casting Wall Street as Victim, Trump Leads Deregulatory Charges," *N. Y. Times.com* (November 27, 2017). Casting Wall Street as Victim, Trump Leads Deregulatory ...*The New York Times* https://www.nytimes.com › 2017/11/27 › business › fina.

Grimsley, Kristin Downey. "Revenge of the Temps: Independent Contractors' Victory in Microsoft Case May Have Wide Impact." *Washington Post* (January 16, 2000), at H1.

Hawking, Stephen. "Stephen Hawking predictions: Human extinction to global warming."
www.cnbc.com/2018/03/15/stephen-hawking…

Heath, Joseph. "Fractional Investors Stoke Stampede: Ability to Buy Shares of Pricey Names is Hit With Millennials." *Washington Post* (July 12, 2020), at G1.

Ismail, Salim. "Why Algorithms Are The Future of Business Success," Growth Institute (last visited Nov. 23, 2021). https://blog.growthinstitute.com/exo/algorithms.

Julian, Mark. "Conservative Politicians Put Blame for SVB's Collapse on 'Woke Capitalism,'" *Washington Post*, March 15, 2023, at A17.

Katz, Margo Sanger. "Democrats Ask Supreme Court for Quick Decision on Obamacare," *N.Y. Times* (January 3, 2020), Democrats Ask Supreme Court for Quick Decision on …The New York Times https://www.nytimes.com › 2020/01/03 › upshot › demo…

Kiernan, Paul. "FTX's Fall Halts Push for Light Oversight." *Wall St. J.* (November 28, 2022), at 23, FTX's Fall Halts Push For Light Oversight PressReader.com https://www.pressreader.com › usa › the-wall-street-journal.

Knowles, Hannah, Natanson, Hannah. "Moms for Liberty, at 3, Now Has Lock on GOP's Ear." _Washington Post_ (July 2, 2022), A1.

Krugman, Paul. "Transaction Costs And Tethers: Why I'm A Crypton-Skeptic." *N.Y. Times* (July 31, 2018).

Lashinsky, Adam. "Crypto is a Solution in Search of a Problem." *Washington Post* (May 22, 2022), at A27, Opinion Crypto is a solution in search of a problem *Washington Post* https://www.washingtonpost.com › 2022/05/20 › cryp…

McGinley, Laura, Cha, Ariana Eunjung. "Conservative Group Sues FDA in Bid to Revoke Approval of Abortion Pill." *Washington Post* (November 19, 2022), at A4, Conservative group abortion-pill-lawsuit.

Melling, Louise. "Religion is no Excuse to Discriminate." *Washington Post* (September 8, 2022),

When did religious belief become an excuse to discriminate? *Washington Post* https://www.washingtonpost.com › 2022/09/07 › supr...

Milner, Yeshimabeit, Traub, Amy. "Capitalism and Algorithmic Racism," 6, https://www.demos.org/research/data-capitalism-and-algorithmic -racism (2021).

Newmyer, Tony. "Cryptocurrency Everywhere-Except in the Cash Register." *Washington Post* ( January 12, 2022), A14, Cryptocurrency is suddenly everywhere *Washington Post* https://www.washingtonpost.com › crypto-versus-cash.

Mohanty, Prasanna. "Rebooting Economy I: Why Stock Market is Booming When Covid-19-Hit Economy Sinks." (July 2, 2020), www. businesstoday .com, Rebooting Economy I: Why stock market is booming when ...Business Today https://www.businesstoday.in › . . . › Economy Politics.

O' Brien, Matt. "Bitcoin Shows What Libertarians Get Wrong About Money." *Washington Post*, January16, 2018, sec.A12, Bitcoin is teaching libertarians everything they don't know ...https://www.washingtonpost .com › wonk › 2018/01/08.

O'Donovan, Caroline. "Uber and Lyft Spend Hundreds of Millions to Win Their Fight Over Workers' Rights. It Worked." www.buzzfeednews.com /article/carolineodonovan/...

Hampton, Liz, Factbox: U.S. oil and gas regulatory rollbacks under Trump https://www.reuters.com › article › factbox-u-s-oil-and-...

Johnson, Akilah. "Studies Find Partisan Politics Can Affect People's Well-Being: Researchers Find Americans in More Conservative Areas Don't Live as Long." *Washington Post* ( December 20, 2022), at A1, Can politics kill you? Research says the answer . . . *Washington Post* https://www .washingtonpost.com › health › 2022/12/16.

Khan, Lina. "Amazon's Antitrust Paradox." 126 Yale L.J. 710, 717 (2017), Amazon's Antitrust Paradox, The Yale Law Journal https://www .yalelawjournal.org › pdf › e.710.K...

Long, Heather. "The Final GOP Tax Bill is Complete. Here's What's In It." *Washington Post* (December 15, 2017), The final GOP tax bill, explained—The *Washington Post* https://www.washingtonpost.com › wonk › 2017/12/15.

McGregor, Jenna. "Gig Economy' Not a 9–5 Replacement." *Washington Post*, September 25, 2018, at A14, How much people really make in the 'gig economy' *Washington Post* https://www.washingtonpost.com › 2018/09/24 › how..

Mooney, Chris, Mufson, Steven. "Why the Bitcoin Craze is Using Up So Much Energy"—

    *Washington Post* (December 17, 2017), https://www.washingtonpost.com/news/energy-environment/wp/2017/12/19/why-the-bitcoin-craze-is-using-up-so-much-energy/?utm_term=.0e3c7f8610f0 (December 19, 2017).

Nelson, Jennifer. "How the Texas Power Grid Works and Why it Failed," https://www.investopedia.com/texas-power-grid-5207850.

O'Leary, Lizzie. "The Anti-Kruman, The Anti-Krugman Libertarians at Sea." Bloomberg Businessweek, September 30, 2019, at 48, The Libertarians on the Anti-Krugman Cruise Just Want to . . . https://www.bloomberg.com › news › features › a-wee...

Neiman, Melissa. "Motorcycle Helmet Laws: The Facts, What Can Be Done to Jump-Start Helmet Use, and Ways to Cap Damages." 11 J. Health Care L & Pol'y 215 (2008), available at http://digitalcommons.law.umaryland.edu/jhclp/vol11/iss2/3.

Rampell, Catherine. "How Regulation Can Be Pro-Market." *Washington Post* (September 11, 2020), at A19, Please regulate us, beg companies that Trump keeps ...*Washington Post* https://www.washingtonpost.com › 2020/09/10.

__________. "Texas's Freeze Exposed the Danger of Deregulation." *Washington Post* (February 23, 2022), at A 25, Opinion | Republicans fearmonger about regulation, but ...*Washington Post* https://www.washingtonpost.com › 2021/02/22.

__________. "The Dark Side of the Sharing Economy." *Washington Post* (January 27, 2015), at A17, The dark side of 'sharing economy' jobs *Washington Post* https://www.washingtonpost.com › 2015/01/26.

Regnier, Pat, Dwyer, Paula. "The Sudden Unmaking of Silicon Valley Bank, Bloomberg Businessweek," March 20, 2023, at 29.

Regnier, Pat. "Well, That Was Weird: Tendies, Game Stop, Silver, SPACS. What. The. Hell.: A Sane Person's Guide to a Bonkers Stonks Market." Bloomberg Business Week, February 8, 2021, at 44, Well, That Was Weird Magzter https://www.magzter.com › Bloomberg-Businessweek.

Rogers, W. Sherman. "Building Social and Human Capital in the Black Community by Increasing Strategic Relationships, Cooperative Economics, the Black Marriage Rate, and the Level of Educational Attainment and Targeted Occupational Training." 17 Hastings Race & Poverty L.J. 211, 229–230 (2020).

Available at: https://repository.uchastings.edu/hastings_race_poverty_law_journal/vol17/iss2/3.

__________. "Occupational Licensing: Quality Control or Enterprise Killer? Problems that Arise When People Must Get the Government's Permission to Work." 10 J. Bus. Entrepreneurship & L. 145 (2017).

*Available at:* https://digitalcommons.pepperdine.edu/jbel/vol10/iss2/1c.

Rosenfeld, David. "The Impact of Insider Trading on the Market Price of Securities: Some Evidence From Recent Cases of Unlawful Trading." 44:1 J. Corp. L. 65, 67 (2018), "The Impact of Insider Trading on the Market Price of Securities ...Northern Illinois Universityhttps://huskiecommons.lib.niu.edu › clglaw › clglaw.

Rotblut, Charles. "Reddit, Robinhood, and Lessons From the Meme Craze, an Interview Spencer Jakab Author of The Revolution That Wasn't, Gamestop, Reddit and The Fleecing of Small Investors." *AAII Journal* (April 2022), at 7; Reddit, Robinhood and Lessons From the Meme Stock Craze American Association of Individual Investors https://www.aaii.com › journal › article › 16673-reddi..

Rubin, Gabriel T., Harrison, David. "Proposal Aims to Regulate Gig Workers." *Wall St. J.* (October 12, 2022), A1, Biden Rule Would Add More Gig Workers to Company ...https://www.wsj.com › articles › labor-department-pro...

Saeedy, Alexander, Biswas, Soma. "FTX's New CEO Faults Lax Oversight in Bankruptcy Filing Wall Street Journal" https://www.wsj.com › articles › ftxs-new-chief-says-com...

Schwartz, Oscar. "Untold History of AI: Algorithmic Bias Was Born in the 1980s," *IEEE Spectrum* (Apr. 15, 2019), https://spectrum.ieee.org/tech-talk/tech-history/dawn-of-electronics/untold-history-of-ai-the-birth-of-machine-bias.

Shaban, Hamza. "Bed, Bath & Beyond Enjoyed a "Meme Stock" Resurgence: Shares Soar on Digital Plans, Partnership With Kroger, Buybacks News." *Washington Post* ( November 4, 2021), at A 26., Bed, Bath & Beyond enjoys meme stock resurgence *Washington Post* https://www.washingtonpost.com › 2021/11/03 › bed-...

Siegel, Rachel. "Reports Shred Banking Controls: Fed Seeks Tighter Reigns After Crisis," WASH POST, April 29, 2023, at A1.

Sisson, Patrick. "Housing discrimination goes high tech." *Curbed* (Dec. 17, 2019, 6:12PM EST), https://archive.curbed.com/2019/12/17/21026311/mortgage-apartment-housing-algorithm-discrimination.

Straight, Brian. "Do gig workers want to be employees? It depends who you ...FreightWaves" https://www.freightwaves.com › news › do-gig-worke...

Van Broekahoven, Haley. "SEC Proposes New Rules to Protect Retail Investors From Wall Street Sellers." http://www.theracetothebottom.org>rttb>sec-propo...

Vaughan, Liam. "Is it Luck or Insider Trading," *Bloomberg Businessweek* (October 4, 2021), at 47, Is Stock Market Rigged? Insider Trading by Executives Is ...Bloomberghttps://www.bloomberg.com › news › features › is-sto.

Verspille, Allison, Beyoud, Lydia. "Bring on the Crypto Regulators: If FTX Had Followed Existing U.S. Rules, Many Customers Would Have Been

Protected and it May Not Have Imploded," *Bloomberg Businessweek* (December 12, 2022), at 20–21.

Weixel, Nathaniel. "GOP States Tell Supreme Court to Wait on Reviewing Obamacare Case." *The Hill* ( February 3, 2020).

Will, George F. "Can America Do Big Things Again? Ask the Regulators." *Washington Post* (June 16, 2022), at A21, Can America 'do big things' again? Ask the regulators and . . . Marshall News Messenger https://www.marshallnewsmessenger.com › can-america-...

——————. "Witness How Progressives Forfeit the Public's Trust." *Washington Post.*

Whalen, Jeanne. "Amazon Joins Race for Quantum Tech With Caltech Center." *Washington Post.* (October 27, 2021) at A18, Amazon joins race for quantum computer with new Caltech ...*Washington Post* https://www.washingtonpost.com › 2021/10/26 › ama...

Yerak, Becky. "Is Marco Rubio Right About 40% of Banks Wiped Out by Dodd-Frank?," Is Marco Rubio right about 40% of banks wiped out by ...Chicago Tribune https://www.chicagotribune.com › business › ct-rubio-do..

Zakaria, Fareed. "The Populist Plutocrats March On, *Washington Post.* (December 1, 2017), sec. A21.


## Articles Without a Specified Author

"About NYC's Most Famous Building | Empire State Building," https://www.esbnyc.com/about#:~:text=Construction%20was%20completed%20in%20a,1%20year%20and%2045%20days.&text=Beautiful%20inside%20and%20out%2C%20the,marvel%20beloved%20across%20the%20world.

"Algorithm," *Tech Terms,* https://techterms.com/definition/algorithm (last visited Apr. 30, 2021).

"Anti-Helmet Issues"—*Bicycle Helmet Safety Institute* https://helmets.org › negativs.

"Artificial Intelligence vs. Machine Learning: What's the Difference?" Northeastern University Graduate Programs › graduate › blog › artificial-intelligence -vs-machin...

"Bank Failures Should Not be Routine," Editorial, WASH POST, May 2, 2023, A18.

"Congress Approves First Big Dodd-Frank." Rollbackhttps://www.nytimes .com › 2018/05/22 › business › cong...

"Congressional Authority to Regulate Abortion"—*CRS Reports* https: //crsreports.congress.gov › LSB › LSB10787

"Employee Versus Independent Contractor"—*Digital Media Law* ...https: //www.dmlp.org › legal-guide › employee-versus-...

"FDIC Government Regulations Resources," https://www.fdic.gov/regulations /resources/cbi/report/cbi-full.pdf

"Mandatory Helmet Laws—Freedom Or Safety Issue?" *EatSleepRIDE* https: //eatsleepride.com › mandatory_helmet_laws_-_f...

"SEC Charges Kim Kardashian for Unlawfully Touting Crypto" . . . https: //www.sec.gov › news › press-release › 2022–183.

The Greenlining Institute, "Algorithmic Bias Explained: How Automated Decision-Making Becomes Automated Discrimination,"19, https: //greenlining.org/wp-content/uploads/2021/04/Greenlining-Institute -Algorithmic-Bias-Explained-Report-Feb-2021.pdf.

"The Law of r/WallStreetBet"s https://www.butzel.com › alert-The-Law-of -r-WallStre...

"Trump Rollback of Civil and Human Rights Regulations," https://civilrights .org/trump-rollbacks.

"22 Good Things That Happened in 2022,). *Washington Post,* Editorial (December 25, 2022), at A18 ( Number 20 titled: AI is Having a Moment), Opinion|22 good things that happened in 2022.

*Washington Post* https://www.washingtonpost.com › 2022/12/19 › goo...

"What is the Trump Administration's Track Record on the Environment?" https://www.brookings.edu/.../what-is-the-trump-administrations -track-record-on-the-envoronment.

"What Are Algorithms? A Guide to Algorithms for Children." *Juni Learning* (Sept. 2, 2019), https://junilearning.com/blog/guide/what -are-algorithms/#:~:text=An%20algorithm%20is%20a%20set,or%20 solving%20a%20particular%20problem.&text=The%20recipe%20for%20 baking%20a,all%20examples%20of%20an%20algorithm.

## Scholarly and Other Books

Anker, Elisabeth R. *Ugly Freedoms*. Durham, North Carolina and London: Duke University Press, 2022.

Bentham, Jeremy. *Theory of Legislation*. Trubner & Company, 1871, 4th ed. 1882.

Bork, Robert H. *The Antitrust Paradox*. New York: Free Press, 1978.

Conard Alfred F., Knauss, Robert L., Siegel, Stanley, *Agency-Partnerships*. Mineola, New York: Foundation Press, 4th Edition, 1987.

Dukeminier, Jesse, Krier, James E. Alexander, Greogry S., Schill, Michael H. *Property*. New York: Aspen, 2008.

Harrison, Jeffrey L., Theeuwes, Jules. *Law And Economics*. New York and London: W.W. Norton & Company, 2008.

Harrison, Jeffrey L. *Law and Economics in a Nutshell*. 5th Edition, 2011. St. Paul Minnesota: West Publishing Company, 2011.

Krugman, Paul. *Arguing With Zombies: Economics, Politics, And The Fight For A Better Future*. New York and London: W.W. Norton & Company, 2020.

Morris, Virginia B., Morris, Kenneth M. *Standard & Poor's Guide To Money And Investing*. New York: Press, Inc., 2006.

Nichols, Cheryl. *Broker-Dealer Regulation*. Durham, North Carolina: Carolina Academic Press, 2017.

Rogers, W. Sherman. *The African American Entrepreneur: Challenges And Opportunities In The Trump Era*. Santa Barbara, CA: ABC-CLIO/Praeger (2019).

Rogers, W. Sherman. *Winners And Losers In The American Capitalistic Economy: A Primer*. Columbia. Maryland: Colmar Publishing, 2016.

## Reference Books and Miscellaneous

Knight, Wesley. Sermon titled, "The Choice is Yours—A Word on Abortion," You Tube (May 21, 2022).

"Dystopias: Definition and Characteristics," *Read Write Think* (2006) (PDF)

"Definition of Dystopia," *Merriam-Webster Dictionary*. Merriam-Webster, Inc. 2012.

Genesis 2:9.

Revelation 12:7.

## U.S. Constitution

U.S. CONST. amend. I

U.S. CONST. amend. II

U.S. CONST. amend. IV

U.S. CONST. amend. V

U.S. CONST. amend. V

U.S. CONST. amend. XIV

## Legal Cases

303 Creative LLC v. Elenis, 6 F. 4th 1160 (10th Cir. 2021), *cert. granted*, ___U.S.___ (February 22, 2022), final decision at 600 U.S. ___ (2023).

California v. Texas, 593 U.S. ______, 141 S. Ct. 2014 (2021).

Dirks v. SEC, 463 U.S. 646 (1983).

Dobbs v. Jackson Women's Health Organization, 597 U.S. ___, 142 S.Ct. 2228 (2022).

Halliburton Co. v. Erica P. John Fund, Inc., 573 U.S. 258 (2014).

In the Matter of Cady Roberts & Co., 40 S.E.C. 907, 911–912 (1961).

King v. Burwell, 576 U.S. 473 (2015).

Massachusetts v. EPA, 497 (2007).

National Federation of Independent Business v. Sebelius, 567 U.S. 519 (2012).

SEC v. Texas Gulph Sulphur Co., 833 F. 2d. 833 (2d Cir. 1968), cert. denied, 404 U.S. 1005 (1971).

Sharette v. Suisse Intern, 127 F. Supp. 3d 60 (S.D.N.Y. 2015).

Superior Bath House Co. v. McCarroll, 312 U.S. 176, 180–81 (1941).

United States v. O'Hagan, 521 U.S. 642 (1997).

# ABOUT THE AUTHOR

P*rofessor W. Sherman Rogers* is professor of law at the Howard University School of Law School in Washington, D.C. Professor Rogers is licensed to practice law in state and federal courts, including the U.S. Supreme Court. He is also a registered stockbroker and general securities principal, and has life and health insurance licenses. His multidisciplined background as a law professor, practicing attorney, stockbroker, and life and health insurance agent has provided him with a great deal of practical and theoretical knowledge in the area of law, entrepreneurship, and economics.